the
other
side
of loneliness

Also by Ned O'Gorman

Poetry

How to Put Out a Fire
The Night of the Hammer
The Buzzard and the Peacock
Harvesters' Vase
The Blue Butterfly
The Flag the Hawk Flies
5 Seasons of Obsession: New and Selected Poems

Nonfiction

The Storefront:
A Community of Children on 129th Street and Madison Avenue
The Wilderness and the Laurel Tree:
A Guide for Teachers and Parents
on the Observation of Children
The Children Are Dying

Anthologies

Prophetic Voices: Ideas and Words on Revolution
Perfected Steel, Terrible Crystal:
An Unconventional Source Book of Spiritual Readings
in Poetry and Prose

the
other
side
of loneliness

a spiritual journey

Ned O'Gorman

Arcade Publishing • New York

FIRST EDITION

Library of Congress Cataloging-in-Publication Data
    O'Gorman, Ned, 1929–
    The other side of loneliness : a spiritual journey / by Ned O'Gorman. —1st ed.
        p. cm.
    ISBN 1-55970-795-X (alk. paper)
    1. O'Gorman, Ned, 1929– 2. Educators—United States—Biography. 3. Children's Storefront. 4. Urban poor—Education—New York (State)—New York. I. Title.

    LA2317.O335A3 2006
    371.10092—dc22   2005032877

Published in the United States by Arcade Publishing, Inc., New York
Distributed by Hachette Book Group USA

Visit our Web site at www.arcadepub.com

10 9 8 7 6 5 4 3 2 1

Designed by API

EB

PRINTED IN THE UNITED STATES OF AMERICA

To Cass and Nick Ludington
and to
Joe Keller

Contents

Part One

1. Southport   3
2. The Grandmothers   30
3. Chicopee Falls   38
4. Bradford   46
5. The Neighborhood Playhouse   70
6. St. Michael's College, and Then, Love   79
7. The Community of Christ the Redeemer, 1954   96
8. Hopeless Hall   106
9. Europe   132
10. Mount Saviour   157

Part Two

11. Ricky   171
12. Harlem: The Beginning   178
13. Harlem (Continued)   188
14. Harlem Stories   197
15. The Sensibility of Misery   213
16. The Person of Fear   218
17. A Possible Solution   223
18. Last Trip to Rome   228
19. A Gathering Up   232
    Poems   *236*
    Coda   *249*

the
other
side
of loneliness

Part One

Sunt lacrimae rerum et mentem mortalia tangunt.

(Our life passes. The world goes on its way. The people weep, and our hearts are touched.)

— Virgil, *The Aeneid*

1

Southport

I REMEMBER BUT ONE HOUSE BEFORE SOUTHPORT, a
jerry-built, meandering yellow cottage at the bottom of
a hill on the edge of a wood in Stamford, Connecticut.
When I was no more than two and a half, I crawled
away from Lydia, my Swiss nurse, after she had begun
to bathe me in a porcelain tub on the lawn. I had
strayed into the middle of a dirt road when, suddenly,
as if a grid had covered the sun, an oil truck rolled over
me on its way to a neighbor. I was so small that it did
me no harm, but I remember looking up into the un-
dercarriage. No one in my family believes this ever
happened, but it was my first memory; gentle but terrifying, beneficent, threatening, august. The truck passed;
Lydia came, scooped me up, and set me back down in
the tub.

Beyond that house, in the center of a wild field,
was an abandoned shack, inhabited, Lydia told me, by

a madwoman. We went there for picnics, and when I grew older I walked up onto the collapsing porch and peeked into the windows. I never saw her, but I was certain she saw me.

The fullness of memory begins in Southport, in an eighteenth-century white wooden house on the harbor. A privet hedge ran the length of the lawn behind a picket fence. The front door was painted bright red, and a bronze knocker shaped like an eagle in flight was bolted to the center panel, hovering, polished to a fierce veiled gold in the fish-laced, salty air.

It was a simple sea captain's house. To me it was a place of mystery: alcoves in the sitting room that gulped in the light, closets under the stair, a servant's stairway, pantries filled with wicker baskets, vases, gardener's tools, and jars of jam and honey, wide-plank floors, rooms that had no shape but welcomed the seasons, their shadows, and their infinite manifestations of the sun, its heat, its arctic edges; in that house my mother and father brought the legend of their love, their beauty, their rage, their tragic kin.

I remember certain shapes, colors, and objects with particular intensity, as if they were blooded runes, live, signs with the garb of being. The dining room wallpaper was a pattern of small yellow and purple flowers; a wainscot went round the room, prim wood, painted white, with a narrow curved molding running along the edge; on the mantel two dusty, ruby-brown silver-topped decanters, with three concave sides, mulled the light, sequestering it. When I was asked to sit with my parents for a formal Sunday lunch, I watched them mass the light when the going got tough, and Father, in a rage at my bad manners, would bring the weight of a heavy silver knife handle down on my wrist when I had set my elbows on the table.

Limoges, Sèvres, and Dalton china dishes stood on end along the fluted shelves of an oak corner cupboard. Fired with birds and flowers, golden drums, garlands of roses and violets, bees, sprays of ivy, fleurs-de-lis, and medallions of swains and shepherdesses, they bloomed with a perfection of art and fancy. One plate, a burnished design of strange russet and blue blossoms exploding in a field of light green leaves and grasses, stands now on a chest in my room.

Father's crest was everywhere: a crown floating on a coiled rope; a mailed fist thrusting up through the crown, straddled on one side by a lion, on the other by a unicorn. Mother's crest was modest: three fusils on a blue field below a coronet, ringed by the order of Saint-Esprit. Both crests were incised into finger bowls, onto sheets, on the scalloped edge of pillowcases, on the flat of spoons and forks. Mother's crest, etched as if by a feather of a knife, reposed with especial glory on a silver teapot with a neck like an egret and a handle curved upward from a niche behind the lid, which was carved from a single piece of ebony.

In the room between the hall and the sitting room (the middle room, my father called it), my uncle, Count Allain de Bouthillier-Chavigny, designed a bay window that Mother filled with flowers, glass jars, and plants. It opened out onto the lawn and gardens. I sat on a great sofa during the searing hours of my childhood, watching the world there, calm, healing, a kingdom where my body and spirit wandered in safety. In a golden frame over the mantel was a painting of Great-grandfather's racehorse Reluisant, prancing across a paddock, the family silks hoisted from a tower on a stable. He seemed a dragon to me, haughty, nostrils flared, sleek pelt and tail reflecting the light of what I knew must have been a brilliant summer day.

The woods behind the barn were landscapes of the certain dark and sweet perceptions about the nature of life and sexuality. In the spring they were gardens of crocus, bluebells, violets, new moss, daffodils, gentians, ferns, rocks, worms, birds, and trysts of boys and girls whose parents we did not know. We were warned away from them, but they beckoned always.

All I desired was somewhere in nature; in the woods, in the trees, in the light, in the fabric of the stone fences, in the roots of trees that tunneled down into the earth like roadways into the underworld, in the arc and thrust of the swing, in the gardens, in the shade of the privet hedges. Beyond a stone wall where forsythia grew in the spring with gold-spined vehemence, in a tangle of willows, giant pines, arbors, and overgrown paths, the widow Lacey and her brother lived in a house of darkened windows, crumbling porches, and an exotic decay, like the cottage of my memories of Stamford. I made forays there, secretly, in the summer to pick wild blueberries I sold on a little table I set up at the top of the road.

One afternoon I went alone and knocked on Mrs. Lacey's door. She opened it and asked me to come inside, for she had gifts, she said, she wanted to give to me. The house was gray with age and decay and a dalliance of mortality and a certain distinction of confusion that only breeding can give to neglect of body and surroundings. On a round table, polished and graceful amid the clutter, she had set a glass of milk, a plate of biscuits, a bouquet of phlox, and a globe. I did not know how she knew I would visit that day. Had she watched me on my blueberry burglaries, had she seen me walk slowly across the paddock outside our kitchen (for she could see our house from her living room), leap the stone wall, and head for her door? Had she quickly prepared the gifts and the food? In the corner, quietly sitting on a rocker, his hands folded on his lap, was her brother, a slight gentleman in flannels and a sweater.

The lawns around our house ended at the foot of a stone embankment. On a giant maple tree Father had hung a swing. I loved to pull it to the top of the embankment and let myself soar out over the grass and flowers, high, so high, I thought then, that I could see the sound and the sailboats on the surface racing into the horizon. In the center of the lawn, near the garden and my mother's peonies, a lilac tree, barren each year but for a few blossoms, stuck, like Tasso's oak on the Janiculum in Rome, out of the ground. When I was little, I climbed it. It seemed very high then. Once I fell from it and gashed my chin. As I grew, it never grew any stronger. I watched it from my window in the snow and in the spring rain, a sentinel in the world around me that trembled with chaos, of permanence, of eternity.

Roaming about with shovel, spade, and rake, basket

and shears, Charlie, our gardener, tall and thin, a ruthless illiterate, commanded the small but perfect world of Mother's garden. He brought his craft and fury each spring when he called forth from the rigid earth narcissus, crocus, daffodils, and the first russet shoots of peonies. I was a creature of the seasons. From my bedroom windows, I saw on one side the harbor, on the other, the garden, the hill, the swing. I recall with clear, sensuous, ringing immediacy each hour I spent out in that perfect world. The earth, the trees, the smell of the salt air, the garden paths, the overturned soil, the bark on the trees, the gleam of the bronze eagle on the red door, the fence, the privet, cling to my nerves, to my sense of taste, of touch, as if, had I the courage and the faith, I could summon them back, out of time, to the table before me.

My parents possessed our house with their youth. I remember them as fragile, winnowing apparitions of perfect physical beauty. Mother was a Doric pillar in her isolation and muted, almost ice-cold fragility. Father was a charioteer, opening and closing doors, distracted always as if he were about to undo a plan or reset a post in the ground. He had no bodily presence to me, but a sleek, rambunctious, wicked, spiritual one. He seemed as if he would rather be somewhere else, inhabiting another world. He dreamed quite beyond the reality of his wife and children. He maneuvered through us as if we would attach ourselves to him like ticks. Mother told me that Father was terrified that he would grow old and lose his youth and beauty. When he was thirty, he told my mother, it was all over.

Sam and Annette (my parents) greeted guests, after a day of sailing or riding, in the front hall, beneath a silver and copper lamp hanging from the ceiling, holding within a crystal bowl three bulbs that sent sheaves of light across the walls and up to the first landing of the stairs, where I used to perch, watching it all like a spy. I remembered the feet of their pals in riding boots, sparkling evening shoes, and sneakers, tramping through that bright red door, tramping snow, manure, and fresh-cut grass over the rug. The scents of perfume, stables, liquor, and the harbor rose to my perch, heralds of the life that I lived, wrapped round in a coat of many colors.

I was wrapped always in a curious lamentation, fired with the most exquisite sensuous delights. I went to bed at night with the rattle of demons in my blood, but awoke the next morning with the greatest expectations of pleasure and delight. I lived in the spell of the seasons, and the harbor that ran its course outside my window bore me with it when I could not block out the assaults of a bewildering, intoxicating frisson of terror that rose out of the battles my parents waged incessantly with themselves and their friends. One morning, after a night in which the house resounded with a bitter hullabaloo, I looked out the windows before breakfast and saw Mr. Lacey, with a bright and jolly swagger, cross the street and walk out onto a jetty that shot off from a wild bit of land he owned next to the water. He jumped into a sailboat, hauled up a bright red sail, and drifted past our house toward the sound. I looked out the other window, and Charlie walked down the garden paths, bending now and then to touch a flower, straighten a stem upon a lattice, and gently prod the turned-back, wet, brown dirt that had delivered up to the late spring morning the first great blossom of a scarlet peony.

Father was always a boy. He never grew up. He stormed at me with a primitive affection, swinging me into his arms, ruffling my hair, tossing me on a horse at the age of seven, staring down at me with hot misgivings, but never stopping long enough to notice the color of my eyes. I spent my time trying to outfox him, escape his vigilance. When I was not in school, and Father was at home, I spent much of that time on Taintor's Hill. Father could not get me there. I was safe from him, for I was in terror of his footstep, of his hands, of his entrance into a room. He had no fondness for my nature. He found me effete, too thin, too meager for his boundless, cradle-like ego. I knew Father could have crushed me with a glance. I had to stay clear of him. I knew nothing of what he ever thought, and a child who cannot read his parent's mind is at the mercy of all his nightmares. On Taintor's Hill, I was simplified and happy.

Had the order of the day been in Father and Mother's hands, I fear I might not be alive now. The household was held together by our nanny, Lydia Hoffman, who was the human heart, my sounding board, the engineer, the keeper of the keys to order and to sanity. My parents floated above me, around me, with their love and piteous marriage, but they never caught me in flight. They leaned on the light of beauty and youth, and I tumbled through them like water. Lydia was the ballast.

She had immigrated to Brooklyn from Switzerland, married, and somehow found her way into our family. She treated us all like sacred beings. When my parents' marriage had disintegrated, when the bank was pursuing Father with summonses for bounced checks and mortgage payments, Lydia went through the day as if nothing was out of order. She polished silver, ironed my mother's nightdresses and underclothes, waxed the furniture, prepared our meals, served them, and kept fiercely to her own sense of mortality, which meant that we were forever at the mercy of her rages, her quiet, intense hatred of my father. (Once, in a rage, she threw a full shaker of martinis at his head. She missed, but her fury did not.)

Lydia was an ethical force. She set my younger sisters, Annette and Patricia, and me against one another, favoring one, rejecting the other. She lorded it over the kitchen, making it a forbidden place we entered in fear, but once there found it a haven. She knew the passion of the great unreasoned feelings of love. She was primitive, almost wild. I do not know that she could write or read, but she had a great sense of "possession" of the O'Gormans, as if we were her tribe. My mother told me that when we were very young, and a new nurse was hired to care for us when each of my sisters came home from the hospital, Lydia would drive her out; she would not share us with anyone. She spoke little of her past. She came from Zurich, and recalled that one day when she was a child, the house she lived in had burned down. She placed that house within a walled village in the hills, and her memory of it and the fire was brutally vivid. She stood in a window and watched the village go up in flames. The flames, she said, had almost reached her when a ladder shot up out of the dark and a hand guided her onto it and down to safety. No village in myth, no Troy, no Atlantis, was ever as vivid as that Swiss one, burning, and a child in a white nightdress (she said she felt her dress go up in flames).

Father and Mother and their tribe of friends favored liquor, horses, picnics, and the shared intimacy of a flawed optimism. They were the privileged children of the 1920s, who had been spared any existential hazard. They were cursed by a languishing, feverish sadness, like one sees painted on the faces of Meissen shepherds and shepherdesses, gilded from toe to brow with garlands but empty within, shattered at the slightest touch.

Nightly, from my perch on the landing of the front stair, I watched my parents at supper. I could not hear them but saw them clearly through the screen of darkness of the hall, gilded, delicate creatures: Mother like a votary at one end of the table; Father, glistening, curly black hair at the other; the fire from the candles, the darting figure of Lydia in her evening uniform of black and lace, serving them from glittering silver

dishes. Youth had come in a flash, a gilded flash, a dazzling eruption of beauty, sex, family, children. The
space beyond was seething with death, with the disso-
lution of feeling, the decay of love, and the crippling
shudder of the end of youth. Once I tried to follow
them to a ball, hiding in the trunk of the car, but Father
discovered me and hauled me out. There was no following them.

I remember nothing but his lurching, constant, weight-
less presence. I do not remember his face, his height,
his voice (did he ever speak?). He had his task to do,
and he had to do it in silence. I remember his being
there: all about me, even when he was not there, he
was there, rooted in my small body's inner space, im-
placable as my father's rages, as my mother's habit of
beauty. I awaited him, during those years of his presence in our house, as if he were my dog at the foot of
my bed, my nanny in her white starched apron at her
duties, my father on his horse off to a hunt.

I do remember one thing: his hands, his long thin
fingers, the hair on his arms, his mouth, his mouth especially as it moved over me tough as sand, soft as mud.

The staircase that went from the front hall to the second floor was interrupted in its ascent by a landing,
where I used to sit and watch the comings and goings
of my family. It was an observatory. I could be alone

there, and I cannot remember a time, as I sat on a hard wooden bench that jutted from the wall, that anyone ever passed me by.

But one night before sleep, I sat there in my pajamas and dressing gown (I called it my wrapper) and watched, as I often did, my parents at dinner. The fire gleamed on the silver, and on the night he came to sit beside me, there was an empty place at my mother's right. And then, there he came, silently and tarried, George S. I could see my parents, who had turned toward the stair, for they had heard him begin his descent. In an instant he had untied the cloth string on my pajama bottoms, let himself linger on my flesh. He got up, went down the stairs, greeted my mother with a kiss, and sat down to eat. I retied my pajamas and went up the stairs to bed.

I was the object of his desire. It was never a matter for me of a combat between good versus evil. I waged no battle. Neither did he. My will was subjected to his hands, to his stealth, to his ferocity. I could not say yes to his advances. I could not say no. I was his perceived captive. He was my unperceived, but felt, tyrant. He had settled in me like a wrecked ship.

What I marvel at now is his skill, his tactics of possession, his stealth, his certainty that nothing would ever be revealed, that he would never be "caught."

In our house, there were comings and goings of all kinds of folk: Lydia; Marie, my mother's lady's maid; Charlie; my grandmothers; cousins, aunts, uncles, and weekend guests. Yet George was able to reveal himself to me as he wished, and did with my body what he wanted. Never a slip, never a miscalculation. Rock certain he was, and he mastered me, my house, all my world, and accomplished it all as if he were invisible.

A man who desires boys counts with cruel knowledge his power over the silence of the possessed. I knew nothing of the flesh. I was seven years old. I did not know what he sought. I could not name what he did. I had come upon, about that time, my father's collection of strange pamphlets. I opened a drawer in his bureau where he kept his handkerchiefs. I admired them, so stiff and perfect in his suit pocket, and wanted to touch them. As I lifted one I saw thin, steel-blue pamphlets, and in them pictures of such impossible curiosity that a primal landscape was touched by a certain flush of strangeness.

And of course there was the grace of my life. It absorbed George S. and his dalliances. I had the garden, my father's hunter, Leigh-ho, the seasons, my soldiers and baseball card collections, the sailboats in Southport Harbor, my bike — I was consumed by a miscellany of natural joys. His hands could not reach there.

But he was relentless in his pursuit. In the summers, my father rented an immense old house near a beach on Long Island. George followed us. The little club we belonged to had rows of cabins where we changed into our swimsuits. Suddenly he would appear on the sand near us, and when I went to change, he would follow. I wonder now what my parents knew. (Were George and my father lovers?) In the cabin, with its gray-painted walls, slat floor covered with sand, and white pegs on the wall where we hung our clothes, he would kneel before me, lay his hands upon me, and then suddenly I would hear him shout a muffled kind of grunt, a sharp cry as if he had been hit in the stomach. He would rise from his knees and leave. I would stand there, pull on my trunks, and rush to the beach, where he sat with my parents, drinking and laughing. I ran into the water, the salt, the waves, the sun casting their cool net about me.

I was thin, lazy, and given to fantasies. I had begun to develop, like a massive scar, a violent, wrenching stammer. Poor Father had to sit about observing a child who hated sports, wished for nothing more than to be left alone in his room with his collection of shells and rocks. When I spoke, I shamed Father with an eruption of wounds that held no word in its guttural struggle with meaning. I flew into rages, drove my fist through windowpanes, and sulked. Father could not decide what to do. He presented me with baseball bats, deep-sea fishing gear, a football, a football helmet. I stood before him at night as he forced me to read to him aloud. Perhaps he hoped my stutter would vanish, like a boil popped with a pin, if I just coaxed out the demon. He sat staring up at me, his pipe pricking the haze of my terror, eyes like coals. I screamed out words; they fell from my lips in shatters, a broken pot of maimed sounds. Wizened portions of meaning grew in me like bloated, dead animals.

I was not a religious child. I was a pantheist, a common, unenlightened one, for I was never clever in metaphysical matters, who brought everything, parental skirmishes, sex, god, Meissen bowls, my baby cup, my sisters, my grandmothers, all into a great game with divinity. I played that game all the time. Father and Mother sent me each Saturday morning to Saint Joseph's Convent for religious instruction. I asked my teacher, a hefty nun swathed in veils that had the scent of starch and a raging cleanliness about them, what my soul was like. She led me to a window, parted the lace curtains, and pointed to a bride walking up to the church on a red carpet. The wind had caught her veil, and it floated like a cloud behind her. "That," she said, "is what your soul is like." I tried to fix my soul in my body. I thought of it as a piece of white, fragile paper soaring about from head to toe, kept in my skeleton and within my flesh by the weight of my body.

When I received my first communion, I sat in the pew with my classmates and dreamed the most vivid scene. I was ashamed to talk about it to my parents, but I saw within the landscape of my mind a vast outdoor promenade, and at the end of it, on a hillock, Jesus rested on a stone. He was more like Pan than judge, but he was, I knew, God, a charming god, not threatening me with hot pokers, but rather a calm creature of a rustic sort, a local creature I might have met on a walk through Taintor's Hill.

The Catholic Church, in the days before the Second Vatican Council, was for a disordered, sensuously playful, selfish boy a dominion of enormous and friendly majesty. I inched toward poetry quite alone, scared of nearly everything that hinted of the adult world. Within the church I wandered, touched the fringes of the mystery of my burgeoning flesh and spirit, and never felt hostage to the traps laid for me by my parents and their battle to survive their love. I do not know that the church I love now, in her guises of chic and "relevancy," in her political life, in her hard-boned common sense, could have sustained me, were it the church I had to grow up within. That old church drew me from the abyss into the luxurious life of symbol and myth.

In a household of diminishing joy and the end of a marriage, I sharpened my wits and savored peace while the walls shook with torment. I loved to watch Father when he returned on weekends from his outings with Gold's Dragoons. The day of the hanging, I waited on the front stoop for him to ride up the street, dismount at the gate, and lead Leo, his great mare from the bloodline of Man O'War, into the paddock. Gold's Dragoons were well-placed young men who loved horses, certainly as much as they loved their wives. They dressed themselves in beige britches, scarlet jackets, chains of silver epaulets, wide-brimmed hats with chin straps, black leather boots, and dazzling spurs. Each Saturday they met on Greenfield Hill and rode about in imitation of the drills and cavortings of the cavalry. It was just Father's style: romantic, boyish, absurd, and an imitation of some other life, better, past, and useless.

On the afternoon of the hanging, I waited till Father had sat down to lunch with Mother and his old pal Tony Laudatti, and bolted for Taintor's Hill. It was my room, that hillside, my playground, my church. I climbed the stone fence that separated the hill from the forest beyond and wandered into a stretch of pines and groves that was forbidden land for me. Just over the farthest slope, over a wire fence, was the slum of Southport, rows of dingy houses inhabited by children we were not allowed to know. Once I had seen a boy and a girl undress and lie down in the tall grass that grew up around a little pond we skated on in winter. I knew they had come from that part of town; I dared not look at what they did, but my soul stretched when I saw them vanish laughing into the green.

I came to a shaded ground, damp with patches of moss, and lay down and looked up at the sky. Suddenly they were there, standing all around me, five of the toughs from the village. One sat on my chest and hauled me to my feet after he had struck me on the cheek. He took a rope from a sack, flung it over the branch of a tree, and formed from it a hangman's noose. He said he would hang me soon. I had no reason not to believe him. They made me stand beneath the tree, fitted the rope around my neck, tugged at it so that I had to stand on the tips of my toes not to have it cut off my breath. In between the heaves of the rope, I let out thunderous shrieks, and just when I thought the end was to come I saw my father bursting through the trees, epaulets crackling in the sun, his scarlet coat like an arrow. When the boys saw him swing his great hat in the air like a shield before him, they fled. I dropped to the ground, and Father carried me away weeping in his arms.

Can I be certain that what I have remembered is accurate? The child in me is dead. I write of his resurrection. I seek cause, find effects, and call them causes. I seek the past, find the present, and understand it as past. What seems to have been appears to me as certain, and what appears as certain seems often to be the fiction of the moment. Has time delivered history and memory from the coils of reason, so that what I observe now is, in fact, what can only be true: memory in the cauldron of error, of fantasy, of fact, of grace?

At the bottom of Harbor Road, propped up on salt-battered, ancient pilings, was a dock, and around it a gentle grace of a lawn. Our family used to go there on the days the Atlantics were racing, to watch them return like sullen swans from a tangle with a maelstrom. On the Fourth of July, the village gathered there for the fireworks that shot up from a boat a mile or so out in the sound. I watched the sky shake and crack with fire and the spasms of color and darkness. I smelled the fish and the clams and, through the darkness, smoke, gunpowder, phosphorus, burning.

This is the story — myth? — I learned of my mother's family. My maternal grandmother, the marquise de Bouthillier-Chavigny, was a Florentine of a minor branch (probably from the wrong side of the bed of the house of Savoy). She married my French grandfather when he had inherited his title and fortune and moved with him to Canada, where he bought a hermitage, raised racehorses, and went bankrupt. He moved his family to Cambridge, taught French literature at Harvard, lecturing to ladies in Cambridge about the lives of the marquise du Deffend and Mlle de Lespinasse (his kin), about Lamennais and Gallicanism, Mme de Maintenon, Lacordaire, Père Didon, and the glory of France. He died at forty. He distrusted Americans, who, he wrote in a diary, "walk everywhere and sit with hats on in public cafés." He distrusted Harvard, thought it atheist and common. There was a photo of him standing behind a fire grating, hand on a silver-topped cane, monocle, held to his waistcoat by a white ribbon, in his left eye. On his finger, a ring with his crest carved into a sapphire. He is dressed in a gray suit with a stiff white collar. In his buttonhole, a white rose. The apartment of Aunt Gilberte, my mother's sister, was filled with family runes and tatters settling there like silt from the river of a dynasty's decline. Family chateaux, surrounded by lush gardens, deep moats, and towers winged with pennants and vines, women's faces staring down out of gold frames, women so beautiful they could not have lived save in a time when perfect beauty simply survived and could be inhabited — worn like a perfect linen shirt, the world David painted, the world of my aunt, Madame de Richmond. There she sat — a great favorite of visitors to the Metropolitan Museum — on a gilded chair, at her feet, head on her lap, her daughter, golden hair and a perfect, aristocratic face. No hint of age in mother or daughter. They seem to be cast there in the screen of gentle light like leaves from a blossoming rosebush cast on the grass by a gentle wind: detached, reflecting magnificence, a momentary intrusion in the world. When David had finished their portrait, the girl went out to play, and a horse, frightened by a sudden storm, pulled loose and trampled her to death.

My maternal grandmother, Nana, dressed in long, shapeless black dresses. She wore a veil that reached to her knees; at the crown, like a low fire, a sapphire and diamond half-moon hid among pleats of tulle. She smoked three packs of Lucky Strikes a day. She told me of her life in Paris, of nights in the family box at the Opéra when the light was seeded with jewels and the Royal Guard lined the grand staircase, their white plumes still as marble in the luster of the gas lamps and candles. Often in the winter, late at night, Nana stole into the stables of l'Hermitage and drove to the house where her husband kept his mistresses, hauling him back before dawn to keep his indiscretions from the

children and servants. Once, a cousin told me who remembered hearing the tale from a stable hand, when
she crossed a frozen river just beginning to melt in the
last days of winter, icy water seeped into the sleigh and
she felt it splash about her ankles.

Her sons, Guy and Alain, were the fiery nonpres-
ences of my childhood. They were in the shadows of
conversations, passing like hot coals through the
household, and in the pieces of myth and history I
picked up from my kin. How strange those myths and
history are; when I tell my mother that I heard these
tales, she tells me that I must have concocted them or
dreamed them up. (But I know *someone* told me that we
were kin to the house of Savoy; Uncle Percy, my father's brother, did tell me about Great-grandfather
O'Gorman's mock Greek gallery, and another of
Mother's sisters, Aunt Yvette, *did* tell Aunt Gilberte
that she was part Blackfoot Indian because of a liaison
with an Indian girl her grandfather had; I remember
Aunt Gilberte going into a swoon when that tale was
recounted when I visited once in Aunt Yvette's apartment in Greenwich Village.) Well, myths or not, Uncle
Alain did sell his title, and designed part of the interior
of the *Normandie*, and worked as an assistant to Lady
Mendel. When I saw them, they seemed beautiful,
weak, sensuous, usually drunk, and very sad. They
died young and poor. Life appalled them. They had no
court to dally in, just the brutal cities of the New
World, where their careful gait and measured style was
drawn and quartered. There was something in their
necks, in their hands, that seemed to me strange and

badly assembled. They went to Harvard, did their military training at Saint-Cyr; one designed a three-cent stamp. I do not think they ever spoke to me, nor I to them. But they were part of the world of heroes and bums I adored.

On the walls of Nana's apartment were photographs of Mother's family: Uncle Alain, the vicomte dressed in the regalia of Saint-Cyr — gleaming helmet, plume, breast plate, epaulets: radiant, apart, mute. An aunt of Nana's, her head swathed in a white starched cap, high bands of linen round her neck, sits on a chair with giant studs of gleaming metal along the arms. (She looked to me like a fox.) In the center of them all is a photo of l'Hermitage. Scattered among the trees and lawn are Grandfather's family, visible now, standing as if waiting for the perspective to devour them. In one picture, on the seashore, Grandfather stands in the middle, surrounded by all his children, swimming in a mist in which time, or the photographer, or the sea, had submerged them. Grandfather's horses, in a brown frame carved with roses, hang near a copy of David's painting; the marquis is there, holding the reins of his favorite horse, hand on hip, surveying the world as his grooms hold the horse's neck high.

Nana told me: You are of noble blood, my child. There would be kings in this family were it not for . . . (I cannot think why there would be kings; had it something to do with the unlucky assassination of some ancient cousin in the sixteenth century?) I did not believe or disbelieve her. She added just one more myth to the chest of them I already possessed. She would walk out of a room if Napoleon's name was mentioned. And meanwhile, across town, in a house on Twenty-third Street, in ruins now, Great-grandmother O'Gorman collected by the shelf-full every image of Napoleon she could get her hands on.

She was wrong about the kings, her children, and the world. She was a lady of the nineteenth century, when the wellborn lived brilliantly, but not without lament. She preserved the values of her class with serene but jealous anxiety. She saw the barbarians over the hill. Piety, manners, and faith were no protection against time and the middle class. During those years, I feasted on that fragile, heraldic dream and lost myself in imagining the life of the abbé de Rancé, our sixteenth-century paternal cousin who founded the Trappists. His life, in all its lurid, penitential majesty, hung in Nana's hallway in the glow of a red light, in etchings yellow and gray with age. In each one the abbé is a figure in extremis: his gaunt body sitting on an abbatial throne, standing amid his monks, dying on a bed of ashes and straw, a man who lusted not after the wrong things but with the wrong gusto. He was a voluptuary, but turned on the flesh when he was a monk and forced his monks to pull up nettles and thistles with their bare hands as signs of obedience and penitence. My French kin were, and are, tight knots of moral sumptuousness and dour piety, rocking back and forth on the thin edge between folly and grandeur. One cousin is an armaments manufacturer, another has a collection of thimbles, worth, I hear, a considerable fortune; one was a cloistered nun; some are bankers; all of them, I know, do not *approve* of the world. Those I love most make wine and champagne, the Chandon-Moët. They are bankers — but they know the glory of the vineyard and are the gayest de Bouthilliers I have met. Both my families find gaiety difficult. The French and the Irish share this — the stumble and whine of doom is always in the blood.

I love one etching in Aunt Gilberte's apartment above all the others. It is the Château de Montmort, with an inscription beneath it by Victor Hugo:

CHÂTEAU MONTMORT, MARNE. CATHERINE DAUGERE.
1567 SULLY DUCHESSE D'ANGOULÊME.
M-SE DE MONTMORT.
Tout à coup en sortant d'un bouquet d'arbres on
aperçoit à droite comme à moité enfoui dans un
pli du terrain un ravissant tohu-bohu de Tourelles,
de Girouettes, de Pignons, de Lucarnes, et de cheminées.
C'est le Château de Montmort.[*]

"We spent our wedding night in that tower," Nana told me, pointing to a window high in the trees that swam up into the heights of the castle from a lawn of sheep and shepherds, fruit trees, and massive stone escarpments.

---

[*] All of a sudden, appearing from among a clump of trees,
one perceives on the right, half hidden by a dip in the ground,
a ravishing tumult of towers,
weathervanes, gables, dormer window, and chimneys.
It is the Château Montmort.

"Goddamn your noble blood, you're an American," Father told me. And it went on like that, as if it mattered.

The O'Gormans and the Irish against the de Bouthilliers, the house of Savoy — I'm certain that alliance never existed but in my imagination, though Great-grandmother was called Marguerite de La Savoie — the Holy Roman Empire and the Trappists and the lot of them against my New England kin, the terrible-visaged Ebenezer Thompson, John Edo, Aurora Farnam, Malachi Bullard, Bethia Breck, and the Blackwells and Darlingtons. (I discovered those kin in some family papers that I found in Grandmother O'Gorman's desk when it was delivered to us after her death.) Only fire, thunder, and calamity could come of such a gathering: England, France, Italy, Ireland, and New England galloped over my imagination as if I were made of tightly packed turf.

Photographs in an old album of my father's show his family at play at their house on Sands Point, a grand house belonging to my great-grandfather in the second half of the nineteenth century. Men, women, and children stand, sit, stroll along the sea, watch boat races, play with hoops, hide from the sun under white umbrellas and in covered carriages. Nurses sit in the background under trees in aprons and caps. They all pause in the sunlight that shines like apple blossoms on their formal outdoor clothes. In each picture, they seem to enter a little more into the darkness of time. They are lined up in the album, soldiers before battle, the enemy behind, their knives turned upon them, nets hovering above, fire and hobnailed boots ready for a bloody stomping. The surface of life was serene, chaste; class, the last resort of the beleaguered sensibility, held back the tide of history with ropes, crested silver, and embroidered linen. They were no match for the cast iron of the twentieth century. The family leaps from those pages like beasts from a gilded myth. They wrestled with death, inert and breathless, while time, the machine, and the decay of feeling covered them with the sands and webs of revolution and the end of the temporal domain of privilege.

A land formed within me, a bizarre, dark, passionate landscape that had the ring of the banshee and the dying king, the mythologizer, the coward, the poet, and the perverse black-tempered bandit. I waged the first embattled explorations over the face of that land with my father, who took hold of my spirit like a dog with a rag bone. Irish and hence without mercy, he loomed in a demi-world of intense love and violence. He crumpled me in his arms, though I felt all the while I was there, his fists were clenched, ready to fall on me if I made a false move. Did he think I was mad? I often thought he did. He demolished all the odds. That tall, black-haired lava of a man tried to whip me with sensual, masculine energy into place. I slipped through all his plans, and the more I escaped, the fiercer he returned, armed with more rigor, more rage, more impossible demands on my virtue. I delighted in the vices that enraged him: indolence, escape from tasks with a book in hand, silence, slovenly care of the horses; that specially angered Father, since he saw the horses as the one task that would rescue me from my rather too silken European manners.

In the perversity of his wit, he had a vision of me as a great horseman. He put me on horses, and I fell off; on again I went, and in one picture I am perched on the back of Leigh-ho, his stallion of the Gold's Dragoon days, looking behind me as if I awaited an attack. I was seven. He wrote this in my autograph book: "To my son Ned, the future master of hounds of the Fairfield hounds."

In the spring of 1942, we moved to Vermont, to get away, Father said, from the German bombs he was sure would fall on New York. In truth, he wanted to get his wife and children into the hills so that he could escape our adolescence, which peered out behind the innocence of childhood. Father saw us coming as clear as any bomb, and ran for shelter. But we would remain there only one summer before Father moved us again.

2

The Grandmothers

GRANDMOTHER CAROLINE SNYDER O'GORMAN WAS A stern, cool, spike-witted, abbess-like wellborn lady, who dressed in black or in black with white polka dots, and wore her hair piled high in tight gray coils. Her voice was sharp and rational. She spoke of love and her children as if she knew neither but on the most restive terms. She let nothing slip by her: manners, vulgarities in dress, in language. I once was caught as I tried to hide from her judgments. In her apartment on West 108th Street, I broke a Ming vase to shatters with a cane as I was playing Indians in the drawing room. She came, summoned by the crash, from her room at the moment I whispered, "Damn." Swooping down, she grabbed me by my collar and hauled me into the bathroom, where she washed out my mouth with soap and water. I tried to hold my nose, struggled to escape the strength of her hands. I could not and swallowed some of the liquid, lukewarm and slimy, and thought I would choke to death. She held my face down as I twitched and tried to scream. The weight of her body's strength and the grappling of her hands had no mercy in them.

She spoke, like all the O'Gormans did, of ways and means, of order and deportment, seldom of feeling. She had been reared in those rigid decades when right was right and wrong was wrong. No gray; no mercy; no joy. Her world was one of luxuriant green and soft rose tints. No thorns; no imbalance; all was ordered and modulated. Tragedy, feeling, sympathy, could not thrive. All her children had received from her blood a wrecked sense of life.

When I visited her in her vast apartment, she received me silently, dressed in black, pearls, and a lace collar, at an oval polished oak table with leather insets. Her collection of ivory elephants strode across a red velvet cloth. She played solitaire on a place she cleared amid a cut glass and silver inkstand, a silver paper cutter, a green lamp, and two packs of cards in a china box, a magnifying glass, and a globe.

In the years before her breakdown, she sat there with patches over her eyes, studying braille. She had been long obsessed with the belief that when she turned seventy, she would go blind. So soon there were piles of immense volumes of Dickens in braille stacked about the room. And she would sit, her hands going over the heavy pocked pages, murmuring, as she did, the text. She loved Dickens and read him to me when I was a boy. I feared blindness too, when I was living in Vermont on my father's farm. I staked out a fence in the upper pasture, and when I went into the barn to tend the horses I tested my vision by looking at it and discerning, I was certain then, that it grew dimmer each day, and I felt the claws of blindness dig into my soul. Even now, in moments of distraction and sensual dismay, I think of that barn, the stillness in the eaves, the horses standing in their stalls in their monumental sleep. I see the fence go gray in the dusk and in a flash vanish into the horizon.

When she died, this woman who made me tremble when she crossed our threshold, in the debris of her estate that washed up on the floor of our library in Vermont were great stacks of Dickens in braille, and boxes of brushes, combs, mops, and brooms that she bought from Fuller Brush salesmen for whom she felt great pity, and when they came to call bought out their entire stock.

On my day trips to her apartment, she planned an excursion for me, always the same. We left her apartment and climbed aboard an open-top Fifth Avenue bus. We rode to Thirty-third Street and got off in front of the old Tiffany's. We walked to look in at a window on Thirty-second Street, where a policeman on a horse, resting in cast-iron elegance, severe as Torquemada, the handiwork of a cousin, had been given permanent locus there by a grateful Tiffany to a good customer. I discovered once that he was a sculptor of considerable note. He followed us in his sexless, cast-iron banality until he vanished with Tiffany glass, tortoiseshell candelabra, silver, fishing poles, and the black leather copies of Dickens in braille into those caverns in the world that gobble up family chattel as they fall out of moving vans, shelves, and trunks. We would then proceed up Fifth Avenue, sometimes by bus, sometimes by foot, to the St. Regis. There we went to the bathroom. The morning ended with a visit to our cousin Roland Knoedler in his gallery on Fifty-seventh Street, a little shopping at F.A.O. Schwartz, and a sandwich at Schrafts.

In 1943, during a week in July, Grandmother's spirit fell dizzily into madness. She summoned my father from the country, and he and I went into the city, where we found her sitting in the dining room of her apartment in a rubble of pots, pans, silver, mops, cans of food, books, paintings, jewels, and linens. I thought I had entered a madhouse. She had fired her maid and gone about her house pulling down paintings from the walls, and had piled them where we found her, as if she had heard that the world was coming to an end and had gathered her belongings for the trek to paradise. She told my father that she was going to die and ordered him to take her to a nursing home. He did, but after a week she summoned him again and came to live with us in another of my father's muddled Edens in Chicopee Falls, Massachusetts, where we had suddenly moved from Vermont a year before, Father having decided to be part of the war effort.

She was a terror, and I remember nothing of her that speaks to me now of love or gentleness. She walked through the light and shadow of my childhood with a sharp tempest-glare. Once, in the garden of a house we had rented for the summer in Old Lyme,

Connecticut, while we were shelling peas, she turned on me with a measured fury when I had forgotten my task and had fallen into distraction: "I am going to disinherit you, for you have a sluggish mind." She was right, but that sluggish mind saved me. There is something to be said for the passive heart. I feared the O'Gormans' uprightness and purity. Such virtues are not right for a child. There is no moral code in a child's universe, no ethics, no aesthetic. A child knows no human trait quite as well as fear. I was much closer to my French kin, who dawdled with their lives.

Richard O'Gorman was my great-grandfather, and I have learned this one great myth about his life. In the nineteenth century, he was banished from Ireland when a plot to slay an emissary of Queen Victoria failed. He was brought to London to trial, for he was the chief instigator and a famous wild man. (He was famous as a Casanova and, so I remember being told, of a sort of assembly of scoundrels and rakes in Paris he was called the greatest of them all.) He was judged guilty and sentenced to hang. But somehow (one never knows the intimacy of a myth's more particular data), he got an audience with the queen, who, bowled over by his beauty, sentenced him rather to roam the seas on a ship until he died. And so he went off. In Turkey, the first port on his journey, he jumped ship, swam the Bosphorus, took up with a lady, lived with her for a decade, and then turned up in New York City, where he became a judge and a politician and a passionate reader of Greek. On a vast piece of land that jutted out into Long Island

Sound, at Sands Point, he built a great crawl of a house that perched on a cliff overlooking the waters.

My great-grandfather loved horses and had a stable of them, but his son, my grandfather, thought only of boats. (Irishmen tend, to their destruction, to think too often of only one thing.) He was persuaded by his son to have built for him a boat, the sort of boat that he had glimpsed in *The Odyssey*, a galley that Ulysses took to sail from Troy to Ithaca, to Penelope, who awaited him in the trap of her loom. When the boat was built, he told his sons to sail with him in the morning, and the boat was launched down the channel into Long Island Sound, as he sat on a chair high on the stern reading aloud to the morning light and to the clam diggers along the way from *The Odyssey*, in Greek. My uncle Percy told me he heard the laughter of the clam diggers when they turned to see such a sight, a fantastic ship, a red-haired old gent shouting out a language they had never heard, and his sons like galley slaves piloting it on as if they entered into day like a dream they had never dreamed.

When they returned to shore and tied up the boat, they walked up onto the deck, where they were greeted by my great-grandmother, her maids, and the grooms under an awning, where a meal had been laid out: for me, as I listened to that tale, my great-grandmother was Penelope; the judge, Odysseus; and my grandfather, Telemachus.

The power of the Irish, their clumsy grace, their childish affections, bore the brunt of the sex, religion, poetry, and manhood that began to flourish glumly, grandly, in me. I think that the countryside of Connemara is the landscape of those years. Wild, barren, shot through with geological mystery, the habitation of the gods and the image of the ironic glories of the world. I took a trip there in 1963. When I looked up at Mount Mave and Ben Bulben and watched the purple fires of the West Country seep into the fields and raise them up in a crystal mist, I thought of my father's family and of their dusky style and affectations. There is more in Father of the gilly and the potcheen maker than there is of the nobleman and knight. Oliver St. John Gogarty says that there is something of the caveman in the Irish. He is precise. Irish silence and cracked Irish nature held the key to my father's secret life and his hardships with love. He would be alone, solitary, creeping out into life — like the gillies, he'd rather be in a wood by a stream than in a drawing room. But his children demanded that he talk and watch them, arrange their lives and support their whims and praise their frailty. So, as soon as he had enough of noise and the presences of kin, he'd drift away and hide. (I thought of him one bleak day when his rage had terrified me, sitting in a dark room of the ruined family castle in Clare, listening to the hounds wailing and barking at the moon, as they did, so legend says, when a member of the O'Gorman tribe died. He'd look well, I knew, sitting there, like a hulk of blasted oak, head in his hands, keening along with the dogs.)

The O'Gormans sailed through life with the simplicity of a very sharp ax. They had the stubborn, icy will of the wellborn and could be peacemakers or the most perverse of moral clowns. My father could not bear in the long run either his wife or his children. His letters to his wife were often pleas for her body, and the sensual cries of agony that my mother would not sleep with him; his letters to us were the wailings of a man who did not know how to love anyone but his horses. No violence, no excess of love, was alien to my father. He was a rigor mortis in me, a sign of dread and a physical immensity that I could not challenge. Once he took me to a raft in the sound, and when I said I was frightened of the water and could not swim, he picked me up and threw me in. I knew I would drown, but when he lifted me up, screaming, I knew it was nothing to him.

Father struggled against the barbarian within him. That barbarian has taken up his son, often and without mercy, and set him down till now into Celtic fires.

Against this Irish drumhead — stiff-necked, violent, visionary swarm of clowning fishermen and revolutionaries — my mother's family, from the coast of Brittany and the gold hills of Tuscany, was set like a banner of crocus and dogwood across my life.

3

Chicopee Falls

*F*ATHER'S DECISIONS, LIKE ACTS OF GOD, had nothing to do with reality. Pearl Harbor had found him ready to fight the Japanese, but he was denied a commission in the navy, and in 1942 he moved us all to Chicopee Falls, Massachusetts, where he worked as a guard in a munitions factory. Chicopee Falls was a campsite on Father's wanderings; it just happened he was accompanied by his wife and children and Lydia.

We moved into a slipshod housing settlement, putting down stakes in the last section of a line of six-room attached houses. Our neighbors were army men and their families from Westover Field. We moved in like migrant lions in search of a forest: Lydia, our Airedale, Peggy, my sisters, Mother, Father, and Grandmother O'Gorman. On the front lawn, a patch of weeds, stones, and cigarette butts, our stupendous black custom-made Cadillac — Father got it at a bargain price from a minister who used it to take his choirboys for rides in the country — was set up on blocks of wood to wait out the war. Lydia cooked, polished glass, ironed sheets, ranted at Father, and mowed the little lawn she urged each spring out of the mud. Father slept during the day and guarded guns at night. Grandmother, like a crippled Victorian doll, drifted through the tiny house, a black piece of gauze, frail and dreaming God knows what dreams. She sat on the wooden garden furniture we bought as if she were waiting for a bus. On Saturday afternoons, she listened to the Metropolitan Opera broadcasts and sang aloud the tunes she knew. (She loved *Carmen,* and I remember her singing "Habanera.") She was on the verge of death each day. I found her terrible and ancient; I shook with fear at the coming of her death and the memory of her rage.

I went to a Catholic high school in Springfield. I was crippled with that wretched stammer, and my face was riddled with pimples. I sat like a condemned man in class, waiting for the nuns to call on me to recite. They never failed to call. I was in the line of march, and though they knew I stammered, I was treated like everyone else. Up the aisle the nuns went: Dick you read, now Sally, now Bruce, and now, Ned, you read.

"Who created the world?"

"GGGod CrCrCreated the wwworld. IIII beeee-lllieve in GGGod the Faatherrr almighttty."

When I finished, I sat down exhausted and wallowed in my ugliness. I had no delusions. I forced myself into life with suffering and acts of will I could barely sustain. My stammer was the flag flying from my grotesque thirteen-year-old body. A nun got a hold of me once in the hallways and declared aloud that she would cure it. She pulled a medal of the Virgin from her black skirt and pinned it on my coat. I tore it off and stamped on it. She slapped me on the mouth, and I left school certain that God would strike me dead. That stammer hovered over me like a vulture. It crowded out light and filled me with the notion that I was mad. I despised my body and my spirit. I loved the world and the mystery of my place in it, but my heart, I knew, was condemned for a time to a formal, savage anxiety.

Father had always wanted to be a policeman. When he was a young man, he asked his parents if he could join the police force. They said no; thundered no. The idea that an O'Gorman would walk a beat and traffic with the herd was intolerable. And Father spent his life playing at this and that, never earning much and yearning, I know, for the intense hide-and-seek of the underworld and the games detectives played. He knew nothing of nuance, reticence, disputation, argument, or discussion. With me, he either burned with rage and struck me down with the frontal attacks of his displeasure or zoomed in on me, loved me to a pulp, ambushing me with kisses and hugs. I tried to get away, but the world was blocked on all sides by my stammering and Father's ambivalent arms. I turned inside my skin like an animal in a cage. I waged war against myself.

Behind one of the frocks of my battlefield, down

the street, behind venetian blinds and Sears and Roe-buck curtains, there was Daliah.

My pimply friends and I used to gather every Fri-day night in Timothy Bidlow's house to play spin the bottle. A boy spun a bottle, and the girl it pointed toward when it stopped was taken into a dark room by the spinner and kissed. We all hoped to get Daliah, a red-haircd, lusty, skinny girl with overwhelming breasts. Her father was a captain in the air force. When I won her, we stumbled through the ritual she'd go through with the next one. (There was some cheating: a gentle push of the bottle when it seemed it would stop in front of a less desirable girl.) We locked the door. She took off her sweater and lay back, bare-chested, on the bed. I lay on top of her with all my clothes on and kissed her and held her breasts until someone knocked on the door and said it was time to stop. It was a mark of her favor if she'd reach down into our pants and hold our genitals. She favored me now and then, but I do not think I knew exactly what I was expected to do. When we heard the knock, she got up, pulled on her sweater, and walkcd out into the room, to return, after a few spins, with someone else.

When I wasn't trudging in the erotic swamps with Daliah, I was in love with Betty Mullins. She was slightly tipped over and had a row of clamshell-gray teeth. Her father was a sergeant. The bottle never seemed to stop in front of her. She eluded our bunch's baser wonder. I turned one day (as boys will in their first loves) and found her sister Rhoda, slightly more tipped over, with yellowish skin and a Veronica Lake bob aslant over one eye. I thought she was a model or an actress. There was a little platoon of such girls. The first one I kissed with ecstasy was Puddentain. When I bent to touch her, as she leaned against the white gate of her house (I had to bend a good way, for she was barely five feet tall), I heard her say, in a paroxysm I suspected was transport: "If you want, you can call me Sweet Puddentain." I thought that was an invitation to an orgy, but I never saw her again.

We carried on in our prefab house like exiled crowned heads. The Cadillac rusted away. Lydia groaned in her Swiss rage; Peggy chased the army up the road; and Father tore in and out of the house, toting his pistols and flashing badges.

I tried to live the life of an Average American Boy. I ate in the kitchen — forbidden us in Southport — joined clubs, arranged dances, edited a little news sheet, and dressed in the height of fashion: loafers, white socks, army trousers, and bow ties. But I dreaded each day. The family, in its various styles of agony, was too large for such a small house. Our dog, Peggy, groaned with nostalgia for the hills. I found my way to the upper reaches of a river to a little cove called Bare-Ass Beach and swam and searched for arrowheads. We were the eccentrics of Chicopee Falls. My parents, for all their assays at the ordinary life, simply became to the folk there more and more bizarre. Mother showed up one day with a true leopard coat that gathered crowds. Aunts, uncles, and cousins rolled up in elegant cars, slipped into the house, carried Grandmother out, and drove off with her, all in a flurry of dogs, a crippled Cadillac, and Father, his pistol hanging at his waist.

I survived by trying to be one of the crowd.

Living alone in a two-room shack at the end of the main street was a retired "sergeant," who gathered some boys of the neighborhood around him. I went along. In the dark of his living room, lit by candles and flashlights, he formed us into a little army. We were pledged to secrecy. He instructed us in battle strategy, had us racing up and down his lawn with wooden bayonets, and told us in hushed tones how to sneak behind "enemy" lines, move in the dark, and camouflage our tents. We kept our club secret and tried to win his approval. He had a box of army insignia — eagles, bars, oak leaves, stars, and stripes — and he handed them out to his favorites. We were tested by crucial tasks he set us. I failed them all. Never got even a corporal's stripe. He was training us, he said, one night in the dark of his house, to take over when the "land was invaded." I told my father that, and he forbade me ever to see the "sergeant" again. I disobeyed and returned for one of his meetings, but the house was empty. The neighbors said he had left that morning. We never saw him again.

In April 1945, Grandmother O'Gorman fell down the stairs. I walked into the hall when she reached bottom. Father, naked, since he had just stepped into the tub, carried her groaning into her room. From then on she dwindled into death. The fire went from her fast. She swooned into an invalid crouch, her icy serenity melting into vegetable silence. The only sound she made was on Saturday afternoons when she lay back in her rocker listening to broadcasts of opera, humming away like a mosquito in a jar. Once the smell of death got to her, she breathed it in deeply. The day she died, I sat outside her room on the floor, waiting for the death rattle. I thought it would sound like the hiss and rumble of a basket of vipers. When she died, it sounded like the burning of dry leaves in autumn. I peered into the room and looked at her dead body. She stared up into the silent room, at the springs of the bed above her, her cheeks caved in, her eyes open, and her hands hidden in the folds of a sheet.

I ran downstairs and told my father his mother was dead. My sisters and I were whisked away into the country. The war had ended, and the Cadillac had been reactivated. The undertaker came when we were out and took her body away. (When my father's sister, Aunt Carol Scudder, arrived that day, she took off the O'Gorman diamonds, five large stones, one of which my mother said was hers, and put them in a covered dish in the icebox. "Undertakers," she said, as if they were the kind of people who would wear white socks with black shoes.) She was buried in the family plot on Long Island. The coffin was loaded on a special train at Pennsylvania Station. In the two cars reserved for my family, about forty people drifted in black and veils; to my eyes they all seemed old, thin, serious, and dead. The coffin was covered with a blanket of red carnations. At the grave I kept my eyes on Cousin Almy, who smoked a cigarette and looked, in her tight black dress, like the angel of life.

The year blundered on, and in the summer we packed up dog, Lydia, and children and set off in our Cadillac for Bradford, Vermont. The poet within had begun its ascent into the world. I clamored for consummation. I sought the poem, love, my Father, bodies, and friendship. I sought the extremes of every fantasy. My ignorance was invincible and erotic.

I brought this tangled self to Vermont, the land of my father's dreams.

4

Bradford

*F*ATHER CALLED OUR FARM PIED-À-TERRE, and he up-
rooted us there in 1945, when I was thirteen. It was a
wild hut, a gridiron.

We made a grand, top-heavy entrance into Bradford in the slush and mud of early spring. Our black
Cadillac, followed by two moving vans, inched up the
hill to our house, resting in a hollow between fields of
potatoes and hay. There was no electricity and no furnace. The rooms were cool in summer, freezing in winter, and the wide-plank floors and doors made uneasy
pacts with ceilings and door sills. Soon Mother filled
the house with the emblems of the tribe — china, silver, colored glass, flowered curtains, and that special
wit and grace she managed to bring to life even when
life was brimming over with sorrow. The dreams and
escapades of childhood found a happy landscape there,
and I rested, lunatic and peaceful, in that simple house

as I had in Southport. Peggy, our Airedale, gave birth each year to her children on the sitting room couch, and when the snow piled up high around the windows and some wisp of heat struggled in from the wood stove in the kitchen, I lay on the Oriental rug, closed my ears to the skirmishes around me, and thanked the gods I was an O'Gorman.

Once we settled down, Father began the final maneuver of his retreat. He saw to certain things before he vanished. He designed enormous stables for the horses he would soon bestow on his son, as tests for his manhood. He coaxed lawns out of weeds and had a trim white board fence built around the fields. He painted the barn red and the house white with brazen blue shutters. The barn and stables were in a state of rot, and nothing is so much the face of mortality as a barn in disrepair. Father had a vision of Pied-à-Terre as a country house in the grand manner. It never was what he dreamed it, but it was a dear and wonderful place, flowers everywhere in the spring, autumn leaves in the fall so bright they took my nerves by surprise each time the hills changed into burnished prisms in October. The pines reigned over winter, and through the windows, on the rugs and over the china and silver, the sun burrowed and rectified even the lamentation in my mother and father's hearts. Father cried aloud each day for freedom. He got a job as a probation officer in the Vermont Department of Jails and was soon all over the state searching out disturbed children. He spent weekends with us, inspecting the way his family managed his dreams. The Irish battle in a wild way; no way to distinguish wounds from healing, defeats from victories, skirmishes from retreats. My parents yearned toward us, and we yearned toward them, but the closer we got to Father, the stronger his hand was on our shoulder, pushing us away.

Our land was tended by Mr. Eastly and Mr. Gring, two raw, granite, seerlike, half-gentle, half-savage Vermonters who knew the land and the ways of cattle, crops, and horses, and little else. It was no peasant wisdom they possessed, though once I thought it was. Vermont does something to the bearing of the backwoods farmer. It cools passion to rusty and dull-nerved passivity. The men are just this side of brutes, and the women, puppets made of flowered prints and bowed heads. A lassitude and ravenous loneliness pushes them on through their lives with feverish irony and agony. Mrs. Gring came each afternoon during the winter to visit my mother. She sat in our library for hours, watching the family go about its business. She simply sat, her daughters Touhey and Dewey sitting on each side of her on the couch, silently, unsmiling, driving us all into fits of conversation. Nothing could get them to go until five, when they had to tend to milking. Then they'd look at one another, take one more tour of the downstairs, and walk up the hill toward their farmhouse, silent, serious, and very sad.

I walked every night to the Eastly farm to fetch a gallon of fresh milk for the family. The trek was a dark and frightening one for me, over the south pasture, across Roaring Brook, up a hill, and under an electric fence. At the top of the field, I looked back at our house, the kerosene lamp's yellow light floating in the windows. The vast interior of the barn, gaping behind the monumental sliding front doors, pierced through the dark to the back field, where an apple orchard bloomed in the spring. It was there in the distance like a temple, ruined, unused, the mark and weight of myth. The Eastly barn was dirty, low-ceilinged, and usually filled with Kenneth Eastly's curses as he booted his herd into their stanchions. There was the smell of hay and oats, and the air was moist with the expectation of milk. I filled my milk pail and trudged back, stopping at the brook to test the dark. I listened for foxes and rabbits, and sometimes, if it was warm, I'd go for a swim; hardly a swim, I'd sit in the water or lie in it, the muds and grass and an occasional fish or toad sliding across my skin.

Whenever Father disappeared, we let down our guard. When he was with us, we were careful to be neat, silent, wary, lest we break the spell of peace that descended upon our household if Father were in a good humor.

He was a fantastic presence: violent, gentle, wise, stupid, agricultural, licentious, paternal, and lonely as a lighthouse keeper. I feared him so much that I pushed furniture up against my door at night when he was at home, to keep him out of my room, for there were times I thought he might beat me to death. We faced each other in fearsome tests of strength. He could not have had a more impossible son. I was a vain grotesque.

I hated everyone. I fought with everyone. I bulged with ego and crystalline sexuality that covered me like a harvest of sorrow.

I attached myself to the beasts to please my father. I tended them with excessive sloth. He boarded old run-down nags from the dismantled farms in the village. I brushed their mangy coats, polished tack, mended fences, and rode the tougher of them through the countryside. I loved to hitch Velvet, my sister's favorite Morgan mare, to a gig and drive over the fields and hills that I got to know as well as Dante knew the valley of the Arno.

When Father praised me on a horse, I exulted. Sons crave their father's praise even if their fathers praise them for the wrong things and for the wrong reasons. I would have loved Father to praise me for my love of solitude and for my love of books. On a horse, I was a boy apart from the boy he could not bear, and he whooped with delight when I cantered down a field in good form.

"You have beautiful hands, Ned, and you sit that beast like a prince." Only on a horse could I rescue my father from his gloom. I tried to break him down so that he'd bless me, and for a time I polished tack until it shone and kept the stable floors clean as the floors of a convent. But soon I got sick of horses and could not bear the intensity of Father's scrutiny. The stables went to ruin. The manure froze half a foot thick on the floor, and I had to pour boiling water into ruts I hacked out with an ax to melt it. Father and I tried once to unclog a manure shoot. I wielded the shovel badly; I stared out into the fields. Father exploded. I caught his eye and thought we'd leap at each other in a bloody embrace of love and hatred.

I remember gritty, primitive nights alone in the barn. When I finished my chores, I climbed into the hayloft and lay down deep in the dusty, pollen-thick air. Night fell fast in the winter, and soon I was so deep in the hay that it had covered me, and the chaff burned my eyes, got into my shirt, and rubbed against my chest. The horses moved in the stalls, the wind came up from the woods, and in winter, snow drifted down through the cracks in the roof. Bats, mice, birds, grasshoppers, and cats shifted and brushed through the dark where I lay, still and rapt, trodden on by the spicy weight of the barn and its ancient, collapsing life.

One evening I fell asleep in the sensuous heat of the hay. I woke up when I heard a thunderous creaking thud beneath me in the stables. I climbed down the hay rack and discovered that Man Mountain Dean, a neighbor's gray farm horse we boarded, had dropped dead and lay heaped in a mass of horseflesh in his stall. I looked at him with pity and bewilderment. I did not know how to deal with a dead giant; like an elephant he seemed twisted in that narrow stall, legs crumpled beneath him in a paroxysm of old, tired death. His pig eyes and hairy clay flesh brooded there, and I had no idea how to move him. He was jammed in; his neck squeezed through the iron bars of the trough, his belly filled in all the space on either side of him. His legs, like the roots of a giant tree, twisted under his belly. The next day two men, with rope, tackle, and winch, dragged him out of the stables, hitched him to a wagon, and pulled his corpse over the fields to the horse burial ground, where foxes took care of him in a jiffy. How violent those wrenchings and tearing of limbs. Long bloody gashes had been made in his flank by sharp, rusty nails that stuck out of the walls of his stall.

In that dismal redbrick high school, Bradford Academy, I learned that the cloister of my family's battleground had given me no techniques of friendship. My parents were misanthropes; an abbot and abbess and their unruly monks. Bradford was no town to accept such odd manners.

New England, for all its icy sumptuousness, is a place of vast and crumbling memories of mystery. There is still the air in the villages and countryside of an economy of feeling and a dry theological wit; the Puritan style manages to break through the imagination now and then, hinting at traces of the Lord, His furious impatience with bad manners, the bluster of the devil, the possibility of erratic judgments to hell, and the small hope of salvation.

I set my will to be someone's friend, and the first possibility I saw was Betty Doyle. She sat in front of me in Mrs. Kiely's homeroom. She became the object of all my desires. Puddentain, Daliah, Betty, and Rhoda of Chicopee were there ready for anyone who came along. I had to set out to conquer Betty Doyle. The first days of my courtship were dizzy ones. I misjudged where she was: she seemed to be in front of me, and I'd find her behind me. She called me from the back, and I found she'd appear at my side. She was, as everyone said, "very smart." She answered all the questions put to her, and wrote in a fine orderly script in notebooks carefully margined. She dressed in wool skirts and fluffy sweaters. I sat behind her in awe of her neck and wrote her notes, begging her to let me carry her books to the bus, to sit beside me at lunch, to talk to me in the halls. I wanted to touch her hair at the nape of her neck and hold her hands in mine. One day she disappeared and never returned to class. A year later she died of tuberculosis in a hospital in Montpelier. For months I could not get it out of my mind that she would turn up again in class. I was haunted by the memory of her neck. She was the first hint I had of the ways of love and its silent, sensuous, and tragic designs.

I had no time for poetry then. I read every book in my parents' library: Balzac, Maupassant, Dickens, Shakespeare, Robert Service, Conan Doyle, and, more wonderful than any, the *National Geographic* and *Compton's Children's Encyclopedia*. Father used to gather my sisters and me in the library, on those nights when he had a revelation of peace and repose, and read in a wild, loud, singing voice Mark Twain and Robert Service. The first poem I really listened to with awe was "The Shooting of Dan McGrew;" it is still to me the cherished song. Grandmother O'Gorman had a partiality for Dickens, and Mother loved *Hiawatha*. In Bradford High School, I remember *Evangeline* and those sinewy, heavy alexandrines. But books were always less sweet than the seasons, and sweeter than any

53

mystery was the new place of women in my life. I told no one of my agony over the death of Betty Doyle. I told no one either about my love of Renée.

Renée was tall, blond, angular, grimly intelligent. She was called by all her teachers "the sweetest girl in school." No rutty, blousy Daliah was Renée. She was tops in everything, especially math, and was favored by the basketball hero. Her father was rich and drove a red Cadillac. The shutters on his house were red. I did not dare dream of knowing her or her family. But I set my sights on Renée and dreamed up some strategies to meet her.

I bolted on a Saturday night from the stag line at a school dance, where I tried to wish away my dreadful sense of awe in the presence of my peers, and asked her to dance. I held her thin, bony frame against me tightly, moving slowly over the floor, her hair beneath my lips, her breasts on my chest, her legs rubbing against mine. Lust rattled in me like a penny in a glass jug. I planned to walk with her into the field and make love. When the dance was over, the basketball captain took her away.

I knew I was in love with something: Renée's body, her face, her eyeglasses, her blond hair. Or was I not in love at all, but like a hitchhiker simply looking for something to carry me away, as she did — and on the dance floor of Bradford Academy, a hard little planet where my jeering friends thought heaven knows what about that fellow trying so hard to conquer Renée! I drove home in a fit of joy. I was tasting love. I'd see her the next day and days after, and we would

exchange glances, for she was in love too, and we'd sig-
nal the erotic lights out of the winter nights. We would
be face-to-face in some fiction, a given divine correc-
tion amid all the horror of the barn and my parents'
desperate sexual blunderings.

The hills struck out toward me in the light of a full
moon as I drove back to the farm, racing up the hill in
the new enlightenment of passion. (On the way up the
hill something darted across the road, and I felt it strike
against the fender. I stopped the car and got out to see
if I had hit a deer. I saw nothing. I looked around the
fields along the road and saw nothing there. When I saw
the deer in the apple orchard, I was certain all was well.)

When I got back to the farm, I heard the old mare
pull at her halter in the stables. I went into the library
and wept. I lay on the couch and thought of Renée for
hours. I could not sleep. The fire in the potbellied
stove was low and warm and banked for the night. I
watched the moonlight in the fields. Was she thinking
of me? Was she in the arms of the basketball captain? I
smiled and thought that this feeling was the most
beautiful thing that had ever happened to me. I was
proud. I was touched by a girl. It was the first sensuous
night I had ever known. This was passion. This was
sex. This was all things, all hills, all waterfalls. I imagined that the next time we met, we'd go into the woods
and fall into a swoon of wild love. I had confused the
idea of love with sex, sexuality with lust, and lust with
friendship, and all of them I confused with life, and
that for a boy is the most divine of errors.

But when I saw her again, there was nothing but

my imagination and her silence. For a year I had the agony of the memory of a night when the affections that had lain so long in a deep agricultural sleep began to kick up their first havoc.

I hated poetry. Keats, Shelley, and Wordsworth wrote of no world I knew. It seemed flimsy, feminine, and a bit breathless. I had no kinship with a poem. I drifted toward poetry in the hills. The gods and the muses sang there.

They sang, too, in Lydia and her strangeness. The sadder she became, the more monumental she seemed to me. She woke in the night filled with dreams and fits of rage. She was possessed for months with the idea that my father had slaughtered my sister and cast the pieces of her body into a frog pond. I looked from my window one winter night and saw Lydia walking up and down the banks of the pond she thought was my sister's grave, calling out to her and swinging a lantern around as she gazed over the surface of the water.

The years in Bradford gave me a manner, a way of going, a strong heart for suffering, and the beginning of a sensuous imbalance, an imbalance that was a crucifixion and a fiery balm. Bradford was a desert and a garden. I was a stranger there, and my classmates knew it and gave me a mock one-way ticket to New York when I graduated. The basketball captain told me I might as well go there and get a job as doorman at the Stork Club.

*   *   *

My mother and father's bouts with sexual love were grim tribulations. These lovers and their wrecked humanity, their grotesque, barely human wailing and lust, were watched by their son with never-ending astonishment, as if they were figures in an ugly circus, traipsing about with their flesh and spirit dangling from them like coils of sea monsters.

Father left my mother isolated in the farmhouse in Vermont, alone with their three children, our beloved nanny, who was becoming madder and more incoherent with each passing day, five horses, chickens, and a car that was in perpetual disrepair. Sheriffs and creditors were at the door with summonses, threatening to cast us out into the fields. My father's stone-cold family sent bits of cash to rescue us. Father often sent us $10 by wire: we'd buy a chocolate cake mix and spaghetti. He bounded in on the occasional weekend, looking for sex, always geared up with a rage that settled like a pole of fire between his eyes. It burned hard the whole day long. (Was that rage a hint of the Alzheimer's that finally consumed him?) But it was Mother he wanted. The sex manuals that he still hid under his shirts in that dresser were, I thought, his guides to genital protocol, and when I snuck a look at them when he left, they were always in a different place in the drawer. He consulted them.

He shouted at my mother in a flint-hard whisper that he wanted her, and when she refused, he accused her of wasting herself on her children, leaving nothing for him. Mother was beginning to drink with gluttonous sadness and refused him her body. One night, however, she crawled across the sitting room floor in her slip, begging him to make love to her. No, he said. No. And once in the library, on a frigid winter night, she looked up at him — they were both drunk — and reminded him that there were days when he could think of nothing but loving her. On and on it went, night and day, their voices drifting up to me as I lay in bed above the library, through a hole in the ceiling that let a stream of warmth into my unheated room.

The house entered into my being. I could not shuck it. It simmered, always, with an animal energy. My sisters escaped on their horses; I hitched up a wagon and drove all day long in the country. Mother had struck up an alliance with gallon jugs of wine, and Father stalked through the rooms and stables looking for flaws in the tack room, flaws in his children's table manners, flaws in our souls — and in mine there were legions.

But there was always the countryside, and I would wind my way, often in tears, to a waterfall and sit naked beneath it, brazen with my companion lust.

There was little for me to do but wander among the ruins. I was the alien, and the memory came to me of George and his hands, and I began to know that love might have something to do not merely with the embrace of the spirit, but with the embrace of the flesh.

To unravel what I was from the apostasies and irresolution, from the conventions and drunkenness, from a family's expectations and their mockery, was a task I could not have taken on had there not been, somewhere, the presence of a healing intervention.

The task of discovering what I might be meant running the risk of scandal, for the terrain was a rubble of surprises, untranslatable since they were deep in the flesh and would surface only when I could not but turn my eyes on the male body that I had found always a vessel of wonder. Once, on a school trip to Canada, I sat next to X. I fell asleep on his shoulder and awoke to find myself watching the skin on his neck. When he turned and saw me, he pushed me away. I sat up straight, touched, I knew, by the slumbering eros that followed me about, breathing upon me in season and out. I was stricken by a cruel, animate imbalance. But then I looked with wonder as intense when I went for a canter over a spring meadow.

Within me, grounded in being, was the homosexual child. I could not call him that, but there he was, scudding about through the days and nights, separate but not separate, within me, beyond me, never colliding with life, but at the center of life. I knew who I was, but that knowledge was dark, brilliantly dark.

Marguerite Yourcenar writes of "a labyrinth in which silence and avowal, text and commentary, voice and echo inextricably mingle and in which disguise becomes an aspect of nakedness."

All the world around me was stricken with a terrible blight. My mother wept and wept; my father, when he was about, stirred up such violence and general mischief that I had to find some way to finish the ugliness off, at least to temper it so that it would not brutalize me.

Then, one shopping day with my mother, I found an escape. I asked her to drop me off at church, at the back entrance, where I could visit the Chapel of Our Lady of Perpetual Help. I told her I would await her there on her return trip home. I climbed the stairs into a hall of offices, opened a door, and walked down a flight of steps to a little cove of silence, candlelight, and the tabernacle. I sat down and looked up at the cross over the altar and at the statue of the Virgin. I cried and shook with convulsions of sadness, a poor, pimply, lusty, broken boy who loved waterfalls, horses, books, and even the forever-ill chickens in the chicken coop.

I returned to the farm on those days with a heart less stricken, for I knew God did recognize my perfection, my imperfection, my splendor. He had to protect me, and He did. I was saved, though I could not say from what, and I think now without remorse or guilt that I was not merely saved from the tears and the sadness but would find, in the arms I lay in and in the arms that rejected me, a sweet salvation. So when the family went to Sunday mass after a week of Father's barbaric thundering, and Mother sat in tears in the front row (Father insisted we sit there), I could lift up my eyes and not weep, since I knew that down the steps of the chapel there was a presence that would undo it all and unspell me from the trances, so twisted and bloody, that I would have to endure for the rest of my childhood.

My father spoke to me about sex as we were pulling down an old chicken coop on the farm. He reconnoitered it, as if he were moving in on Medusa. His hands on a crowbar, he whacked away at beams, tore out nails, kicked over foundation stones, and in between grunts and sweat and a hail of ancient dried chicken dung, he talked of erections, orgasms, masturbation, wet dreams, vaginas, and Sin. The paraphernalia of the body, sexual feeling, seemed to my father matters of grotesque discomfort. He said, ruddy with exhaustion, "When my father told me what I have just told you, I was sick for three days." I wondered why Father had been sick about something I could not find but divine, exciting, quite my cup of tea. (I remember Lincoln Kirstein telling me once that he had considerable trouble with money, never had trouble with sex.)

Once, on a walk, I came to a waterfall I had never come upon before in my excursions. I took off my clothes and sat under the torrent. The woods were still, and the moss on the rocks and the berries in the foliage around me glistened as if lit from within by a radiance that shot from the sensuous quickening then of my every nerve and muscle. I looked down and saw my cock rise up in the shade of that forest stillness. I did not know what to do. Then, suddenly, with no interference of my hand, I saw the world around me so clearly that I thought I'd go blind. I lay upon the rocks until dark; the waterfall curled into the night, the berries and the moss folded into the silence. I dressed and walked through the potato field to my house. I carried a sweetness in my loins and a delicate animal wisdom in my nerves.

The only friendship I established in those days was with Jesus. Father's rages lasted for days: he blasted his fury through the house, never stopping even for the night, when it seemed in sleep he could not but bequeath to me his malignant presence. At Sunday mass, my mother, wiped out by the day's catastrophe, sat head in her hands, weeping. In church, he carried his wickedness even as he prayed, as he walked to the altar for the Eucharist; it lodged, for me, as I looked at him, in his brow, in the squint of his eyes as he pinned me down with his hobnailed judgment. I sat as still as I could in front of the tabernacle, staring into it as if the Lord might pop out, like a jack-in-the-box, touch me with a wand, and force the horror away, plowing it into the ground, casting it into the abyss. It never did vanish, but the grace the Lord bestowed was the idea that it might.

My greatest fear was that Father would murder me. He burst upon my days with a blooded intensity. He seemed stuffed with fury as a goose is stuffed with meal. He never let up: fury packed into each pore, disgust, mere displeasure, even occasional bursts of pleasure or happiness were plucked out of brutality and bore its mien. One night I knew he'd do me in. I fled to my room and pushed all the furniture up against the door, dragging it across the floor, shoving it up in a barricade, pushing paper in the keyhole so that he could not see me if he peeked in. I lay naked in the cold sheets of my bed, trembling. I wondered how he'd do it: a crowbar, a club of wood, or perhaps he'd strangle me or smother me with my pillow. He had mighty hands and could have twisted my head off in an instant. I waited all night for him to break down the battlements, scattering the chest, chairs, and bookcase across the floor, and stride toward me, a brush fire, a grinding stone, burning my flesh, pulverizing me into meal. I still await him, now and then, in my dreams.

Of course I was not a child a father would find easy to bear. I was lazy, bone lazy. The heaviest burden Father had to reckon with from me was my intellectual and poetic bent. I was clearly "going wrong." I collected shells, rocks, built shrines to Saint Thérèse of Lisieux, and thought I might become a priest. My uncles and cousins hunted, played polo and touch football, fenced, sailed, went shooting, and skulked around golf courses, but I did nothing. I languished away with books and poetry. I listened to music and glittered like a cove of fireflies on Father's dreams, biting into this idea of "son." He worried, I know, I might go all flimsy. Father caught me reading one day when I ought to have been working in the fields, uprooting weeds. I heard him as he passed me by as I sat in the sitting room reading Maupassant: "Jesus, Annette, look at him sitting there reading. He's queer."

Persons did not exist for my father. My father was a center, a place, an object. He cared for me, used me, attacked me with brutal and loving regularity, and wished me well. The out-of-doors was the only life I knew, the only thing then that ever possessed me, that I ever possessed. Father, godlike and martial, reduced me to ruin. On the dining room wall, opposite my place at table, a hunting print hung against the blue-cornflower wallpaper. A gent in pinks, coattails flapping, hat secure, fence perilous, was suspended in the air, in hot chase after a fox. When Father was at his bruiting best and bellowing, I extended my will, mounted the horse, and rode off after the fox, the hounds yelping at me, not Father. I'd go so deep into the picture that I lost the family and heard nothing but Father's fist upon the table calling me back into the fray. Father was specially wild at meals; he had us all at hell then, and in arm's reach, and we could not slip away.

I scavenged the seasons. In spring, the fields burst from frozen plains into shallow lakes that exploded with new grass, rocks, violets, and daffodils. Life floated up from the frost; our horses, cats, dogs, and chickens fled into the sun and attacked the world, barking, neighing, kicking up mud, rolling in the new flowers and marshy grass. Their lovely bodies pawed at the spring light, and each time a horse got loose from his stall, I chased him through the fields and led him back, his head tossing and pulling at my hand, to the barn where the smells of the pastures and the cool running of the streams entered and fretted at him through the nights and days, until he was free to live the summer in the open. The first day I could, when winter had slid off the fields and wind, I pushed open the cathedral-high sliding front and back doors of the barn and watched the spring air and brightness rush in, in a wave of thunderous and spicy gaiety. Cords of light fell on the beams and the dust; hayseed and cobwebs shook in the tumult. From the floor and rafters, the winter dark unrolled, and a flood of new life and the smell of rains and flowers in the fields invaded the barn, as if spring were a tornado. In one corner, partly hidden by old crates, trunks, and timber, a nineteenth-century oak table and a beautiful mantelpiece decayed bit by bit into a smoldering pile of termites and ants. The lovely lion's-claw legs of the table had been eaten away during the winter by the damp and cold; the mantel's chaste wooden trim and molding had broken from the heavily carved sides. Moths built nests among the buckling wood and nails and laid their eggs and their dead in slivers of wood and crumbling plaster. Each year, the lion's paws sank deeper and deeper into the dirt floor. On the far hills that rose up from the pastures, the farmers moved out early in spring with their horses, plowing and seeding in the ceremony of planting. Mr. Eastly scattered the seed; Mr. Gring, in front of him, led the horses and plow that kicked up the new earth. Mr. Gring's plow stood in the fields all winter, covered with snow like a ceremonial beast, growing black with rust, but in the spring it came alive and did its work. We all thrived in Bradford by suffering, getting used to being demolished, wrecked, and resurrected.

The air crossed the light like wind across the surface of a still pond. In a carriage of trumpets of seasons, bright pumpkins, pots of zinnias, and burnished waters, the sun followed me, on horseback, on foot, in a surrey. A book tucked in my trousers, I stalked the world that in

October was on fire, ripe and ready for poetry. (I kept lists of new words in my pocket. Most of them were from Henry James and Willa Cather, and a diarist I discovered — where? — Julien Green, whose reflections were the rhymes of my slowly unslumbering soul.)

Winter drew the family in from the world and increased its sorrow and gaiety — gaiety was hanging like a sword always above us. It is difficult to recall those long cold months. If they were just a forced agony of our tormented spirits, it would have been merely a time to remember with horror, but life with my family was never merely one thing. Life was like the bed I climbed into at night in midwinter; the sheets freezing, frost thick on the windows, and no heat in the house, yet we never got colds. Life full of threats, storms, and survival.

Winter diminished the world. Walks were shorter, and the hills covered with ice and snow were no longer landscapes our horses could carry me to when I mourned and wished to flee my father. But we had skis and sleds, skates and sleighs, and to skate over an icy pond, insulated from the sky and sun by a thick wall of pines, was a perfection of another kind, an ascetic, voluptuous, icy delight; monastic, tormented. After a blizzard and a day of thaw, followed by freezing, the woods were transformed into high-ceilinged temples of icicles and green branches of rococo zero-degree solemnity. No sound when I skated round the pool; occasional gusts of wind brought a bit of ice to earth. A winter bird flew to a branch and knocked snow onto my cap, and beneath it all, as the snow piled up, I could feel spring, the flowing streams, the flowers, the worms, the beetles, and the moss inching upward from the frost. A ripple of water pushed through the edges of ice on the skating pond, uncovering grass and, on a warm high noon, a patch of loose brown loam.

Our house then was lit by kerosene lamps. Lydia cleaned them every day, and they shone like crystal. The ceilings above them were burned with circles of soot and heat. The smell of kerosene and wood burning in the furnace and coal in the potbellied stoves are as sensuous in memory as the smell of herbs and raw, freshly butchered meat in towns along the coast of Asia Minor. My mother — always the regal keeper of order and delight — set on shelves in the hall her collection of antique glass: ruby glass, milk glass, ancient green jugs and pitchers. The windows froze over early in November with a heavy layer of frost and remained opaque till spring, when the sun burned out patches of light, melting away the ice from the center of the panes outward, letting the light fall through the lovely red and green glass, as if a curtain had been lifted from a rose window.

Off the hall in the library, a red potbellied stove burned like a pumpkin in a field throughout the winter. I found peace, light, and reason there. On the table between the windows, the Lacy globe and a Turkish plate engraved with a peacock in full sail rested on a red leather top; around the edges of the leather, carved into the wood, were stars, half-moons, and garlands of painted flowers. In the drawers were the potsherds and chaff of a household: nails, flashlights, stamps, pencils, pencil shavings, envelopes, pens, old rings and watches, and when I pulled out a drawer, in the depth of the table, I might find a dollar, a penny, a lost spoon. My mother pulled out a drawer in her dresser and found a ruby and diamond pin lost for fifteen years. We all slept in the library when the temperature fell below zero and froze the ink in the cut glass inkwell in the living room.

In summer life went slowly. The days flowed like wine. We spent hours under the great maple trees, and there the days perhaps flowed too much like wine. Both my parents' families had a dark wish to sleep out their days in the embrace of liquor. They had no tolerance for drink. I heard of uncles dying in Paris gutters and learned the power liquor had over the oppressed heart. I watched a gallon bottle of wine on a red iron table under the oak trees dwindle during the day until it was empty at night. I watched the spell it cast over the loveliest faces and the gentlest hearts. All the style and manner of the house shattered, as if a chasm had opened through the center of the garden, drawing the flowers and the shadows into the abyss. I watched wine overwhelm our family and suck too many of them dry.

That summer, I drove my horse and carriage to a lake in the hills where a giant snapping turtle, by legend a hundred years old, sometimes broke through the surface and sunned itself on the banks. Each morning the dining room table that we had inherited from Grandmother O'Gorman was laden with bowls of blueberries, strawberries, jugs of cool fresh milk, and corn muffins. There was silence, too; the lulls between my parents' wars. The cows came close to the white board fences to nibble the clover on the lawns; the pond beside the house sent threads and rounds of light through the windows and onto the rugs. The gardens brought forth fruit and flowers, and in the sky was the jungle sun, shining through the thickly painted O'Gorman revels.

5

The Neighborhood Playhouse

*I*N THE SUMMER OF 1947, I FELL IN LOVE with the actress Marian Seldes. She dazzled me. I do not think I
knew anything about love then, but Marian was the
presence of love in my life, and I told my father I was
going to New York to study acting in the school Marian
had graduated from the year before. I vaguely thought
I could "pursue" her there. I said that if he did not
send me, I'd smash up my Jeep in despair. Father
dared not cope with his children's neuroses, so he sent
me off, pieces of paper with my name and address
pinned to my underwear, to the Neighborhood Playhouse School of the Theater. (When I arrived in the
city, Marian was away on tour with Judy Anderson in
Medea.)

I knew nothing of life outside the zoo of my family. I knew about fields and waterfalls and the color of
leaves in autumn, and Mr. Gring, the farmer up the

road who tended to our farm, but desire had not been touched by feeling, by the consummation of any passion. I had not touched ground. I boiled along. My stammer sat on my nerves, and my nerves sat on my heart. My journey to the city was a trek toward friendship. I had no friends. Marian became the object of my empty, virgin, stammering heart. I simply had to conquer someone.

(One fall, Father decided to make maple syrup. He ordered his children out into a grove of trees and told us to drill holes in the bark, put in spouts, and hang buckets. We waited. Nothing happened. Mr. Gring told Father that nothing would; we had hung our buckets, he said, on oak trees. I went to New York just as wise about its groves and customs.)

Sanford Meisner's grim, serious, and cutlass-gentle manner dominated the Neighborhood Playhouse School of the Theater. He greeted the first-year students like a dragon inspecting victims for slaughter. Under his gaze, we trembled with awe, for the theater was a holy place to him, and not one inch of this inner sanctum was gained without agony, discipline, and fierce, single-minded dedication. (He knew nothing of my stuttering. I waited for him to call on me to say something.) I was surrounded by curious young men and women, all of them, to me, older than anyone I'd ever known in Bradford. They seemed wise, exquisite, a little dangerous, and very poised. I was still thin, bristling with pimples and innocence. Marian had gone away on tour. I was trapped and thunderstruck. And there was Meisner, ready to cast me into a pit the minute I opened my mouth. I tried to hide my stammer by covering everything I said in a slurpy Irish brogue. What I lacked in eloquence, I made up for by assuming a bon-vivant playboy arrogance. I pretended I was a millionaire and swung up to the Playhouse in taxis as if they were Rolls-Royces. Within, I was paralyzed.

When I had gotten over Meisner, I was confronted with Martha Graham, who was on the faculty of the Neighborhood Playhouse School. She turned me inside out. She was built like a packed trapezoid of nerves, muscle, and a Puritan Wild West spirit, motored by something I understood and feared as erotic and ascetic. She dragged her students around the floor like lightning pulling a kite. I was ashamed of my body. Not one bone was connected to another in any sensible way. Everything flew apart at the joints. Only wonder and an enchantment with this darkly wicked world kept me intact. On a horse, I was in command, but on a polished floor, moving to the beat of a drum and piano, I could not move. I could hear no sound but the clatter of my heart and the breath coming from my mouth like the last gasp of a stricken clown. When the beat struck loud and clear and signaled the class to put their arms up, I'd put my arms down. I was always one beat behind. Or ahead. We dressed in long blue silk trousers, loose at the leg but tight as skin at the hips. I scratched around like a chicken on a henhouse floor. I tried to mimic the tormented spills, leaps, and twists that Graham forced on the will of her students in the early days of her training. I tripped, lagged behind, got lost in daydreams, and fell on my behind. But suddenly I became accustomed to my body. Even when the class, working together on some intricate dance, would suddenly pile up on one another when I lost count of a beat, I felt my nerves lifting their weight slowly off my heart, and I began to bear the heavy albatross of my body less like a curse. I was moving *within* to Graham's commands.

One day I performed a "solo." I pulled a flight of stage steps from a closet, and to the accompaniment of atonal music I climbed them, falling down now and then in my notion of what I thought torment, agony, tragedy, horror, and ecstasy might be. I felt all of a piece, though I must have looked like our old gray boarding mare as she fell in her final sleep, scraping and slithering over the floor. I arched over the steps like a rickety bridge.

Martha Graham drew me up from the static place of my farm boy's sluggish heart and plunked me into the light of my nerves.

The students, paragons of worldliness, walked down the halls brazen as birch trees, though not as gentle. They spoke with confidence of their life in the theater. A blond girl from Mississippi said she'd like to take me home to her mother. A fellow who sat beside me in our history class seemed elegant, witty, worldly, and ungovernably handsome. If only I could manage to be like him. His voice was, to my Vermont ear, intricate, fluid, and high-class. His clothes were exotic, his walk precise yet languid. He moved his hands when he talked, like birds walking a wire. I dared not speak to him. I thought he'd scorn the likes of me. On a Monday morning, his blond hair had changed to flaming red, and I noticed a thin layer of makeup on his cheeks. I took to him less easily after that. I did not know why, but he seemed he had been corrupted a little overnight, and he scared the recluse in me.

Father came unannounced to visit one of Graham's classes. I lay on the floor, spread-eagled, heaving, squirming, bending, jumping, my eyes burning with the presence of such a judge in bulky silence behind me. I had never been so exposed to his vision of me. Martha Graham shouted to a girl who was sluggish in her movements, "Unless you spread your legs wide apart, how do you ever expect to have a baby?" The silence behind me gasped. I had not dared to look at Father, and I knew he was there only because I saw him reflected in the mirror that ran along one wall of the room.

The class went on and on. I wished it would end, so I could take my blue trouser costume-for-dancing off and hide from Father, who would be waiting with some damn thing to say. We stood up together when Graham commanded us and went jerking across the floor in contractions that forced our bodies forward in an arch nearly to the floor. We moved like sheets half frozen in a winter wind. I bent over once — doing rather well, I thought, for a change — but could not get upright. I remained there like a bent crane in a bog as the class continued their movements around me. I tried to hobble off the floor. Father seized me around the shoulders and trundled me like a trained bear down the street to an osteopath, who unhooked me.

I stayed chaste, not because I thought it would be wrong if I did not, but because I simply didn't need anything but the world to enchant me. I was surrounded by all sorts of sexual energies I did not understand; everyone slept with everyone — rather, they "lived" together, and I thought I knew what went on. But if anyone had told me there were "things" going on, I'd not have believed them, since I couldn't dream what they could be. At mass one spring day, when I dreamed of what I knew — the new green in the orchards and the breaking frost under the rocks — I thought perhaps I ought to try my hand at the games my friends played. A boy and a girl had both asked me to live with them. Yes. I said I will live with you. A pain rushed through my head, and I fell forward on the pew in front of me. Sensual awe caught my imagination, and I wished for a moment to be dissolute, violent, possessed. I had no way of conjuring up exactly what I'd do if I "lived" with someone, but it would be arcane and impure. That I did know. I left the church and decided to search out whatever it was I thought I'd decided to search out.

The day was bright, with sun and blue sky. It struck me like a hammer, and a migraine dug into my skull. I returned to the pew and sat shaking and sweating for the rest of mass, looking around me at the few people in the church to see if they knew that I had just been converted to "sex." For a week I walked in a trance, my blood and spirit sour, my eyes misty, my dreams blank and troubled.

My stammer grew in me like a nail. Pimples on my cheeks and forehead, and just a light beard. I could not use a phone, ask for milk at a grocer, or speak to my parents. I had to bring speech and self up out of the dungeon of my throat.

I went to my speech teacher as if I was a crumbling wall; words flaying about in my mouth, expiring at my lips, and entering the world like slivers of mud, turds of sound. I so wished to be fluent, graceful, subtle, but I had a body like a blackthorn stick, a face like an overripe peach, and a heart in extremis. My teacher transmuted my ravaged silence into sound. Each day for five months, she put me through a regimen of tricks and rituals to force the demon to its knees. I stood before her, relaxed my head, forehead, eyes, nose, lips, neck, shoulders, chest, waist, legs, and feet, until I fell to the floor in a heap. I had to get the flesh under control; I was the prisoner, and my body the jail that held language like a bony cell. I read aloud a simple story for children, but one word at a time; each one perfect, unhobbled, simple, itself. I had to breathe through my nose so deeply that my head swam, but the method in this was to find a way to unlock the chains and the bars that had massed like warriors in my nerves.

Then, after a long five months of terror and delight, I was set before my class to speak one entire paragraph alone, facing down the demon for the last time. I read these lines from the Twenty-third Psalm:

Lift up your gates, O ye princes and be ye lifted up. O
eternal gates: and the King of Glory shall enter in. Who
is this great King? Who but the Lord mighty and
strong, the Lord mighty in battle? Swing back doors.
Higher yet; reach higher immemorial gates to let the
King enter in triumph! Who is this great King? It is the
Lord of Armies that comes here on His way trium-
phant.

I cried. My classmates cried. The nail of my will
flew like a banner from the Stammer Demon's head. I
was no longer a mute. The nerves, free from the dungeon, leapt up. I could talk to everyone, ask for milk at
the grocer, and use the telephone. I called everyone;
no longer did a request for a timetable from a ticket
booth at the railway station turn me shuddering into a
stone pillar. A stammerer transformed by his fit goes
rigid with fear, and it was grand to feel so light and free.

I left the Playhouse soon after. I would never be
an actor, and my father simply did not want to spend
money on an adventure that was the vainest and most
expensive of his son's indulgences. I left for Bradford
after working as an usher in a local movie house, rout-
ing out lovers in the balcony. I wore a blue satin suit, a
wing collar, and a red cape with gold eagles and golden
cords whipping across the front. I often stood outside
when the queue was very long, announcing where
there was and was not seating. Once, as I walked up
and down, cape flung over my shoulder, I saw Martha
Graham standing in line with Eric Hawkins. I looked

them in the eye, hoping they'd greet me and call me by name, but they did not recognize me under that mountain of ceremony.

I dreamed each night of Bradford. It was late March in New York, and nothing could still the sounds of the fields and the horses in their stalls pulling at their ropes to be freed into spring.

6

St. Michael's College, and Then, Love

MY FATHER WAS AN IRISH PLATONIST. His children, his wife, his horses, his land, were, alas, but miserable convulsions in the ideal world he would command. In the landscape he imagined, there would be perfection but no passion, no love, no sympathy for anyone in extremis. It was cold, exquisite, bucolic, that backwater of his mind. What he found about him as he built his utopia were the wrecked bodies and minds of his family, in a constant state of mourning under the lashes of his rage. He had opened the door of his imagination and found in the corridors there a vision gone bad, hearts imprisoned, languishing for his love. He scattered us all in the great conceits of his heart.

None of his schemes worked: horses died; four hundred chickens keeled over one night from a plague of coccidiosis; the immense barn doors fell off their hinges; an Adam fireplace rotted away in the dust and damp; ink froze in the cut glass inkwell; and our Airedale, Peggy, gave birth to endless litters on the sitting room sofa. Life was twisted into a knot by Father's fury with it all. He was an earthquake with eyes. No peace, no balance, no joy. We awaited his visitations with terror.

There were hours and hours, days and days, weeks and weeks, when there was no sound not stuffed with weeping, drunkenness, sexual languor, fits of discontent, and screaming, oh, the screaming.

Father could not bear me. I went about my chores: chopping wood, shoveling manure, painting fences, stoking the furnace, and pushing away as best I could the cacophony of the adults that rendered the world bloody and foul. I wept, and when nothing stopped and I could do nothing to stop it, I went into the woods, climbed trees, leapt from the beams in the barn to the hay, where I covered myself and breathed in the scent of grass and flowers and cried, not because I could not bear my parents and their slaughter of a life but because the pollen got into my nose and eyes.

And I fell in love, or so I thought. With my classmates Betty and Jane, and with David, one of my sister's beaux. When he spent the night chastely in the guest room, I grabbed the pillow from his bed when he left and took it to bed with me, clutching it to my naked belly. I would have fallen in love with ducks had they beckoned. For what Father had taken from his children and his wife was love; just that, love, that stark inclination of the heart toward some simple consummation, some elevation of the soul up through the body toward the light. We were beggars. Had Father cast us a stone, we would have received it as manna. But he did not. Not even a stone.

When all his efforts to civilize me and turn me into a proper son, a conventional man, failed, in 1948 Father sent me away to St. Michael's College in Colchester, Vermont. He was a pal of the president of that school, and persuaded him to let me in. Of course Father had no money, or if he did, he let none of it trickle to us, but his charm convinced the treasurer that bills would be paid, and off I went. I took along Father's high-powered hunting rifle (he hunted deer and bear), a silver fork and knife, skates, and snowshoes. I was to escape my poignant jail, but I feared strange worlds. I armed myself. Before I left I went to a grove of young birch trees in a far meadow and nailed a crucifix to the bark of one, near a stone wall beside a stream. I wanted to leave some token behind, to which I could return when the undergrowth in my spirit grew too high and blinded me.

Settled in, I decided I would study psychology. I could not spell it. It had something to do, I thought, with rats running through mazes. And Freud. I was astonished to find that in a Catholic college, before rats and Freud, I had to study God.

And God was everywhere in the curriculum. Prior to the Second Vatican Council, Saint Thomas and his *Summa Theologica* were the source in Catholic colleges of all academic reflections. The saint and his book spilled out in great waves of certainty, order, and truth, verifying existence, entering into the blood, and no matter how Byron and science, astronomy and sex, food and sleep, might seem to have their autonomy in everyday life, somehow Thomist philosophy got in the crannies. It was an itch, and no balm of oils and sin could rid us of its domination. All thoughts were tilted toward eternity and a quest for meaning in the sacred universe. We were all nailed to Saint Thomas, Tun-Belly, as they called him in the thirteenth century. I found it an adventure into language and thought that had never taken up territories in the grand insurgencies of my family; but once I spied the saint, I was an easy conquest.

I went on an intellectual blitzkrieg. That rigid, formal, holy language of Aquinas — form, matter, potency, act, cosmology, proof, the existence of God, and the proofs that got you to Him (the *quinque viae*) — became the base metal of my thinking. He slammed into everything. My room became a stinking den; no one would room with me. Dirty clothes, the stench of vomit (I drank like an accomplished lush). Books lay in piles. I never returned them to the library; they were my treasures, my captives. I smuggled out a manuscript of Bach's *Well-Tempered Clavier* and stared at it, read it, a sacred text, though I could not read music. I read Julien Green, Proust, Leon Bloy, François Mauriac, economic texts, science texts, and I crammed into a box, like little black-and-white fish, scraps of paper with words I came upon in my reading. I took the box to bed with me, clutching it to my chest with the same lust with which I held David's pillow: talismans, runes, objects of desire.

There was nothing to do once I had gotten onto the scent of the world but move in on my teachers. I staked them out. I was ravenous for someone to find me appetizing. No one ever had, and just perhaps, perhaps, that ardor for learning, or learning in its larval state, that I oozed might seduce someone. I followed them as they came to class, far enough behind so they'd not notice me. Which one would give me a map and compass, so that I could wander this new landscape where God preened His feathers, and so that this body I dragged about with me with such insolent brio could be poked into a sensuous bustle with the flesh that would suddenly become coherent and just a little sensible?

I set my sights, first, on Professor Durick, chairman of the English Department. Jeremiah K. Durick was then, to me, a wrinkled ancient, a professor who sat in his office off the landing of a flight of stairs that led to classrooms. He puffed on his pipe with what I knew must be a hieratic purpose amid a clutter of tobacco cans, examination papers, scholarly journals, and books stacked like offerings in a temple: on the floor, on shelves, on windowsills, on his desk. The light came in through leaded windowpanes, small flats of glass that shed a golden vein of beauty on each commonplace. Expectation was everywhere, and holiness and fear, for each morning on my way to class I left him a poem. He took it, laid it on his desk, smiled, said nothing. When would he discover just how bad they were? I waited for a word, for some sound to maneuver its way past his pipe to give me courage. I wanted him to become a muse. He declined.

Once a week, I discovered, looking through a catalogue of classes, he lectured to the seniors on the metaphysical poets. I didn't know what metaphysical meant. I knew Longfellow and Robert Service, Emerson and Whittier. I knew they were not metaphysical poets; it just didn't suit them, that word, so otherworldly. I loved them because I could tramp the world they sang about. I spied the text on Durick's desk — *The Metaphysical Poets*, a thick book bound in blue with gold lettering. I bought it and carried it about with me like sacramental bread. Then, on a dare I made to myself, I snuck into that forbidden class. I took a seat in the farthest row back, the end seat near the door so I could escape if I had to. Durick was already sitting at his desk. He stood up and read from that blue book:

> Where, like a pillow on a bed
> A Pregnant banke swel'd up, to rest
> The violets reclining head
> Sat we two, one another's best.

Pillows? Pregnant? Violets? Bed? Something began to whip round in me, a nervousness of a sort I might feel if I saw a tower begin to crumble in the distance, far enough away so that not a stone would fall upon me, but a sign of catastrophe, a sundering of fabric. And when he lifted his hand high above the book he had laid upon his desk and then brought it down upon it in a slamming motion, reading as he did:

Batter my heart, three person'd God; for, you
As yet but knock, breathe, shine, and seeke to mend;
That I might rise and stand, o'erthrow mee, and bend
Your force to breake, blowe, burn, and make me new.

I was ravished, spellbound, ruined; the ceiling must fall upon me, I thought, for I saw the world as I had never seen it, and it was no longer a place of water-falls, horses, and a mad, drunken family, but a green sward of a land unknown, and once there, once I *knew* I was there, I settled in. I had found a village where I be-longed.

But Durick went on:

Goe, and catche a falling starre.
Get with child a mandrake roote,
Tell me, where all past yeares are,
Or who cleft the Devil's foot.
Teach me to heare Mermaides singing,
Or to keep off envies stinging
    And finde
    What winde
Serves to advance an honest minde.

It all happened, exactly as I have written it down. I could not move from my seat once the class ended. Stu-dents filed past me, Durick the last to leave. He went through the door and into the world beyond that he had forever changed for me. I was not there, but in another room, in another building, in another site. Words hung about me, words I had never heard before, precious things fallen from that blue ark of a book. That was poetry. I had been broken, bent, turned upside down, overthrown. I knew I would never be the same, and never would I again know such astonishment.

It had begun triumphantly, one cold winter afternoon in 1944, as I sat at a table in the library in our house in Vermont. I opened a drawer, took out a piece of paper, and decided I would write a poem. I told myself that if what I wrote pleased me and was a poem, I would be a poet. I took up a pencil and wrote. Snow beyond, sunlight on the carpet. The intricate and delicate carvings of vines and fruit along the edge of the table, the green baize center like a little lawn. The warmth of the Franklin stove, the icicles hanging from the windows. My hand on the pencil, writing. I was there in my enclosed garden. I finished my poem, looked at it, and what I read I determined was a poem. I put the paper in the drawer, shut it, and noticed shadows on the snow and knew it was time to feed the horses, stoke the furnace, and forget about it all until Durick whacked his desk with that angelic, barbarian whack.

When I returned to my room, I wrote a poem, a dreadful botch, but it was a response to John Donne, a take on my metaphysical transport. I dared not give it to

Durick. He'd toss it away, I feared, crash his fist down upon it, scorch it. I brought it the next morning to my English professor, Henry Fairbanks.

> Let there be surcease of flowers.
> O let my head fall down.
> Convey to hell the morning's light.
> Induce from night the tomb of Thel.
>
> Topple into clonic all unperverse joy.
> Deteriorate the clamorous kiss.
> Gouge the hand from roses stem
> and impale the cheek upon the thorn.
>
> Rend to rabble Venus's victory
> of the murderous sea. Rancour!
> Rebellion! Renegade! Rejoice
> in unnatural symmetry.
>
> Doom in dominance will be Redemption,
> deliverance will doom's death be.
> Autochtan of the Heavy Air
> Will enter in Ecstasy.
>
> Echinate, the prickly pear
> is in the temple of the God.
> The commandatore sounds the hour.
> O let there be surcease of flowers.

Fairbanks's response:

Suggest you discipline commendable ability revealed by subjecting same to expression within some conventional (even hackneyed) forms. all aimed at *communication:* the sine qua non of all good writing. is not limited to either the didactic or the ideological; it may be purely emotional but how ever ineffable. it is always understandable. Persistence in current manner will dissipate your best promises. Suggest, to bring power under control, you temporarily use E. Dickinson's poetry (rather than Merton's or Auden's etc.) as model. She is sufficiently modern, or irregular, in form, yet with her infinite variations on old Fourteener, basically traditional. At the same time while eschewing anything of the saccharine and the obvious, she does *communicate,* however elliptically or gnomically.

And then love.

She was erotic, cold, and untouchable. When desire set up housekeeping in my bone, and when I could find no one to rush upon, she became the center of my emotional manner. The daughter of a distinguished scientist at the University of Vermont, she carried to me a sexual flamboyance that to anyone but me would have merely been a quiet and careful grace. No matter that I could never have loved her, no matter that my dreams of Eros were to be cast in another landscape, she became the beloved. I thought she breathed fire, and I lay in wait for her to consume me. I argued myself into her life, waited upon her, grew jealous if she went walking with another, and in a drunken fit I asked her to marry me. I was a poet and would not be able to support her, she said. But nothing could have sated me then, nothing but the infinite, nothing but the world, nothing, no body, no mind, no book. I was interested only in being ravished by something, and Gabriella, in her beauty and sensuous ambiguity, satisfied that abyss of hunger that gnawed at every inch of me.

When her father died, I, and all her beaux, rushed to see her. His body lay in the family's solemn sitting room, head propped up on a little satin pillow, with an attendant mortician popping in and out to dab powder on his face and adjust his hands. The windows were hung with heavy wine-colored curtains pulled tight across the light. Neighbors brought food to the kitchen, and I remember the swinging back and forth of the screen door and the draft that suddenly swung into the room of the dead man, glazing the stillness with a repellent, heavy gloom. The scent of the flowers and the odor of the corpse, and Gabriella silent and weeping, inspired in me a morbid, languorous state of excitement. I was immobilized and kept my eyes on Gabriella, but when I looked at her, I looked at the face of her father. But I cared nothing for the dead man, for we were all there, the swains, to woo a girl who had brought to us our first scent of sex.

Soon after the funeral, I asked her if she would come with me to a dance. I knew she had not the slightest use for me, but she said she would go, and I felt that perhaps I had changed, that the lover in me had suddenly become manifest, and when I gathered her from her house the night of the party I was stricken by desire.

I was a pillar ready to crumble, a pig ready to be stuck, a muffin ready to be spread with honey and eaten. Perhaps I could set her aflame, perhaps I could penetrate the crust that had hardened around my heart.

The evening was a dull, exhausting charade. I discovered that in me there was no love, no desire, just the sham, the empty dawdling: I danced with a ghost, and the crust around my heart curled like a great manacle. I set my teeth on edge, possessed by a spell of sensual madness.

I earned a few dollars a week by tending to the furnace and doing odd household tasks for a ninety-year-old lady who lived down the hill from my dormitory. Since my father had not paid my tuition at St. Michael's, and the school would not cast me out before graduation, I found odd jobs to keep me in toothpaste and beer. At one in the morning on the evening of the dance, I stopped by on the way back to be certain that the furnace was in proper working order, and as I descended the steps into the cellar, there beside the open furnace door, sat the old lady, grinning at me, yellow mucus streaming out between her red-painted lips. Since I had been about the house, she had taken to wearing lipstick and rouge and dogged every step I took. Her tongue flickered out of her mouth, and she hissed at me, clicking her false teeth together. I had the notion that she wanted to kiss me. I shot back up the stairs and wandered the streets till dawn. So, I said in my horror, this is life, eh? Isolation, misery in the things of the heart, and joy and peace stuck somewhere in the cosmos, refusing to descend to me.

Early that night, a young fellow had thrown himself from a bridge into the Winooski River. They fished out his body, word got back to the college that it was mine, and my classmates gathered in the chapel to pray for my soul. Well they might, for I thought I had lost mine, not to water but to desire.

Peter lived in my dorm, an army barrack in a mud alley on the campus. In my room, I huddled with my father's hunting rifle and my jackknife. Alone during the night, I felt him in his room, ready for bed, naked, between the sheets, and yet I could not name it, this lust for him, for his body. Had I seen it, I would have curled up in shame. Sex had no connection with a body then, just with a presence that eluded me as a wild beast might in the darkness of a forest, rummaging about in the bush, there but not there, just the noise of it.

He commanded my soul. I could not know why, but I coveted him, desired him, but I knew nothing of what I desired. I did not know I desired his body. I knew that I loved him, yet I could not tell him so, for I thought I loved Gabriella.

I went into panics of longing. I had no language to explain it all, so I took on curious habits, carrying umbrellas when it was not raining, wearing gloves on the hottest days, dressing like a tramp, drinking, fighting, ranting. I knew that somehow I had to find someone to listen to my tale of desire. I had noticed in the library, working as an assistant to the librarian, a young fellow with a look of kindred longing, and I was determined to talk to him. I had gotten to know him slightly when I checked out books. I did not know his name, but through the clamor of my unleashed soul he beckoned. I went into his office and said (my exact words): "I am in love with Peter." He looked at me and said nothing, and the longer I sat, the quieter he became. He got up, opened the door, and I left. At least now I had spoken, however dismal the response had been, the hieroglyph of my torment, of my delight.

Peter was all my thought, and I never imagined that he might one day be my lover, since I did not know what a lover was. I just knew that he was within me, and I could not shuck him. Had he sprung open desire in me, had his kisses, his touch, readied me for this? I was a clod of carnal misdirections: body, soul, mind, the world, all spun about me, and not a bit of it could I describe, or name.

I wanted to be Peter. He lived in Boston, in the Irish conclave called "Southie," and I visited him there once for breakfast. Suddenly I was there around a table with his family. I felt that I had entered a small Eden, with the beloved body beside me, no fuss, no elegance, no pretensions, just a cunning simplicity. I remember watching him, slim, blond, a marvelous head and a shock of hair falling over his forehead. I thought him an angel. I could not put him out of my mind, yet I could not see him as possessed by me, since the thought of being with him in an erotic embrace had not entered my mind. My desire was lodged, like a sword in a stone, in my head. Only to be with him, to touch his life, to see his parents and brothers and sisters, but I carried with me each minute I was there a fear that if they looked carefully, they might just see how much I loved him. I wanted to capture him and set him down on my body as I would set down a bowl of flowers on a table.

I wanted to cry out across the table: O beloved one, now come to me, wrestle all this desire to the ground, let me — But let me what? If I could have spoken what I felt, it would be babble, since I could not, dared not, scrape the surface of this marvel of love to find a language proper to it.

So I tossed it all onto Gabriella, for whom I had neither passion nor desire: since I could not touch her, I could not touch Peter; since I could not kiss her, I could not kiss Peter. I was drunk in an infinite sorrow with the love of a man and a body I would possess, but since I could not possess him, I pretended to desire Gabriella, and that made it all possible: I could pretend and build a landscape of passion where no landscape existed. The landscape I would wander in turned to a desolate, ugly place, and I mourned mightily, but could not weep.

Delicious it was, this first love, this incredible beginning of desire, of longing, the reflection within my soul and body of a new grace, tattered, mute, flailing about, but urging me on to some consummation.

And then to be a Catholic, in love too with the church, carrying about a condemned desire, though I never thought of it as condemned, but rather as a slightly off-tilt companion to the tribe of desires I carried about in my mind. If I were ennobled by some inarticulate path, it was the path of carnal love and divine love. I never knew a moment of despair when the silence in me did prophesy that Peter would never lie in my arms, but I blustered on in my play-acting, in my innocent deceptions, my fumbling with first poems and then infinite spaces within me that I had yet to explore. Grace shone everywhere.

Years later, I met Peter in a bar in Burlington, Vermont, when I had returned to St. Michael's to hand over some of my correspondence to the library. He had grown fat and was dying of cancer. As I sat with him and some friends, drinking, I wondered if he knew of my feeble love during those blustery days of my passion. Could he not have known? I must have sent out a galaxy of desire, even if it was masked as the false agonies of my unrequited love for Gabriella. He possessed me, I dreamed of him, and in the most grave moments of sleep he washed over me again and again.

I was restless. I pursued the demon in my mindless way, fell in love, drank and drank, fought with everyone who crossed me, and the college, finally fed up, expelled the troublesome creature who wandered back to the farm. Father had left for good. Lydia had gone mad and watched for my youngest sister's body to float down a drain into a pond that Mother had tried unsuccessfully to turn into a swimming hole.

I had heard about another farm in the hills of West Virginia, where a man had set up a community of

Catholics who gathered together, milking cows, tending fields, baking bread, and praying so that they might have a revelation of the Lord, amid the cattle and the fields. I packed my bags and set out, putting the world, the church, desire, and poetry behind me. They were a raging bit of baggage. Charging leviathans. Merciless. I was enslaved to them, delighting in the chaos and expecting everything to be brilliant, agricultural, and ecstatic.

7

The Community of Christ the Redeemer, 1954

$\mathcal{T}$HE COMMUNITY OF CHRIST THE REDEEMER was the sociotheological dream of Kurt Howell. He had bought a farmhouse and 150 acres of land in the countryside of West Virginia and established an experiment in a bizarre utopia, where he beckoned men and women to live out the Christian life under his care. He dabbled in ideas of a rural cosmology and believed he was privy to secrets hidden in the inner lives of those who came to follow and obey him. His ideas were multitudinous, reckless, and, for those of us who revered him in the early days of living there, based on our innocence and the fires of our sexuality, which we held up to him like an offering.

When I arrived, I was given a room to share with an ex-monk, a slim, gray-haired young man with the gestures and a voice of a ripple on a pond: quick, elusive, and formless. He worked, I discovered, at his chores with a formal, controlled frenzy, his body crystalline, taut, flexible. Though I could not have named it then, it was this lusty swagger that bore him up through the days, as if he desired something he could not have, yet was by that desire defined.

The house had a stern, maidenly grace about it, a contrived, chaste austerity. It was very clean. Each piece of furniture was chosen for its simplicity and placed as if it were chattel in a monastery: everything pointed with a planned holiness.

I was looking for a "cell" where I could begin to think, begin to figure out the forms on the landscape of my soul that gathered like animals all about me. I had no idea who I was, but I knew that if I went to a place where I could reach out to that elusive Jesus, then, there, in that place I would find — find what? I did not know, but when I walked into that house, I careened into mystery and loved the smell of it. I had applied for admission as a novice to the Abbey of Gethsemani in Trappist, Kentucky, and was firmly turned down by Tom Merton, who suggested I ought to wait a bit. But that monastic universe would remain a universe I would even now inhabit, though it is a place that will always be alien to the vagabond in me.

I was taken by the ex-monk to the kitchen to meet Mary Arthur, a pretty, chunky girl with ruddy skin, swathed in layers of skirts and blouses, leaning over a table kneading bread. I saw her as a radiant lass, bucolic, cozy, but could not see the ravenous sexual loneliness that would soon overtake her and bend her into desolation.

We ate at an enormous polished table shaped like a cross. Howell sat at the top, silent, lost in his secret galaxy. The community sat along the sides, suppliant and careful always to court his favor. When we finished eating, we read quietly for an hour in the living room. Bookshelves, filled with the thinkers we all looked to for wisdom, towered around us: Christopher Dawson, Jacques Maritain, Charles Peguy, Marcel Proust, Saint Thomas, Paul Claudel, François Mauriac. At nine, we filed into a chapel to chant evening prayers. The room was cold and unadorned but for some symbols of the Christian Mystery hanging on the walls and sewn into a cloth suspended behind a simple wooden altar. I looked up at a fish, the crossed keys of Peter, lines from the psalms, and saints carved from bits of linoleum. I sang with piety and terror. I had left home to seek the church and my dreams of life and poetry. I was overwhelmed with a thudding self-hatred all of a sudden, as if the veil had been torn from my spirit and I saw myself naked, dull-witted, a ragged bit of stuff ready and pleased to be trampled under Kurt's foot.

When I went to bed that first night, David, the monk, said he would wake me at five to help with the milking. He turned out the lights. I was in bed, and he walked toward me across the floor and knelt beside me. He was naked. He lay his head upon my chest. The house breathed around me. Wind rushed at the windows and rattled the frames. He lifted his head, pulled my blanket up to my chin, tucked me in, and went to his cot and lay upon it, still naked, and slept. I stared into the dark and felt a surge of terror and wonder in my body.

At four-thirty, David pulled down the blankets and let the freezing air into my dreams. I washed and walked with him into the barn. The moon was low in the sky; stars were out. The lights on the highway beyond the fields blazed in the barren, frosty dawn. All things in perfect order; not one idea, not one sound, not one smell but glowed with hope. My home, I thought, my home where I will grow and write and love.

The cows ought to have been a sign that something was not as it should have been. Mary Magdalene and Saint Theresa glared at me when I approached them with a pitchfork full of hay. They moaned lugubriously, for, David told me, they had eaten nothing but cornflakes for a month, ever since the day Kurt ran out of money for oats.

It took me some time to learn how to milk. At first I pulled too hard at their teats, and they hit me in the mouth with their manure-caked tails, frozen like lead whips, and kicked me in the shins with their sharp hooves. I learned, though, that it was not just yanking away at their udders that released the milk. I had to become an intimate of the cow's mood, especially since they were hungry on their light diet of cornflakes and an occasional bit of oats. I spoke to them when I entered the barn. I sang to them when I pitched hay into their stanchions. I approached them from the front and patted them on the nose, then slid beside them, placed my milking stool on the floor, squeezed the pail between my legs, and reached gently up to the top of the teats where they joined the bag of milk, put my thumb and forefinger around a little valve I could feel inside, squeezed to release the milk, and pulled my hand down, the pressure distributed evenly on my palm, dragging liquid down the canals in the teat, and if I were lucky and the cows calm, a warm, white needle of milk shot from the udder and hit the pail in a sharp hiss.

I poured the fresh milk into a copper bucket and walked up the path to the kitchen door. The smell of fire and bread bore down on me and the pail in my hand. The house was built on a hill in a countryside riddled with coal mines, stark blasted fields and valleys, and a moral wretchedness thick as the coal gas that choked the air and discolored the light. I stood outside the kitchen door and looked back to the barn. The world from the stoop had nothing in it but genial shadows, contented cows, and the expectation of warm bread in the mornings. I poured the milk into an iron can, sliced a piece of that warm bread, covered it with honey, and stretched out in front of the wood-burning stove. Above me, I heard Kurt walk back and forth, pondering, I thought, the fate of Christians.

I ran like a kite over the fields, in the frost, in the snow, within the sound of roosters and church bells, chasing the dream, the illusion, never stopping to think why it was I could not sleep, or why I turned around fast and walked in another direction when I saw Kurt coming. He walked as if he had a burr up his ass, and he talked with the swagger of a chief clerk. I saw him as Prometheus. He decorated his language with riddles and shot them through with rhymes and reasons he dredged up from our innocent, God-seeking psyches. He made me think I understood him. He needed friends and saw me as a pushover. His language overpowered me: experimental, psychological, "rediscovery of the social character of salvation," "the coming ascendance of social Christianity," "group dynamics."

I was a rat in his laboratory. He suspended any chance of my disbelief with the slippery music of his language and praise that convinced me I was in conspiracy with him against the others, who, he told me, did not "understand."

We all had our hallucinations about the nature of God. God was riddle, reason, philosophy, poetry, and freedom. I rummaged through my mind for solutions to the mystery of the Trinity and the Incarnation. I worked out elaborate theories about the beginning of the world and the nature of thought. When I chopped wood, I spoke to myself aloud, setting out like pots of paint on a table the whole shape of the universe.

David, of the heavy, lightning-like gray eyes, protected me from the searing truths of Kurt's dominion. He took on the worst tasks, sparing me the tedious jobs, arranging that I do a good deal of fence-mending, a task I loved. He dragged logs up hills that ought to have taken the strength of three men. He slung them on his shoulder, head and back thrust forward to balance them, and pulled them to me, where I hacked them into firewood. He loved me with a lusty, measured, erotic devotion. I did not know its sexual ferocity. I growled like a devil at any possibility that I might be loved. I had the mind of a fox and the heart of a hayrack and no wish to yield either heart or mind to any embrace. He was as strong as a bull and gentle as a juggler, his being stripped down to the finest temper. His face was that of a mourning farmer on the morning of a killer frost. His love might have blessed me, but I could receive no blessing. But I do not think, had I given myself into his arms, that he would have responded to my body, too calibrated was his sorrowing flesh, his holiness, his passion. They would be no place for the ecstatic leap.

He saw that I was possibly a man of some intellectual and poetic sensibility, but he also saw in me the wreck I could become. "At times," he told me once, "you are a Thomas Chatterton to my mind, and at other times a mere sixth-rate Gauguin in a phony Samoa. Quit resonating and settle for the role of a sounding board on which others may resonate — else you'll die in a brothel."

On Saturday mornings, I went into town to sell eggs door-to-door. One of my jobs at the center was to clean out a chicken coop that had been unused and neglected for years. Chicken dung had formed a matted false floor of stinking, gluey chicken shit, mingled with feathers and debris. Into that cleaned-out space we brought the chickens that produced the eggs I toted about. Each penny we brought back to Kurt from our sales was a piece of eight to buy the poor cows, Mary Magdalene and Saint Theresa, oats, Kurt stamps and new typewriter ribbons and whatever was necessary to move the center one step closer to that epiphany we hoped was her fate.

The almost sensual power struggle between Kurt and the others festered on. It was like a thunderclap that comes to the point of explosion, then retreats into a dark sky. Kurt, when his schemes seemed balked by our restlessness and laziness and his dwindling bank account, withdrew in smiles and petulant agony into his room, where he'd stay for days. Power was the sickness, and it began to work in us like wind at the edge of a spiderweb. He sought us to give his dreams of power and dominion shape. (We were his storm troopers for Christ.) But we were a dreadful bunch of sexual, religious, intellectual orphans, and nowhere was our home and no one our master. We were lambs, all of us, and Kurt, our slaughterer; we nearly laid bare our necks to him, but were saved in time by our youth and its instinct to survive every demon. We had stumbled into Kurt's arms like lemmings drawn to a sea that would consume them; Catholic lemmings, rushing toward an apocalyptic seashore.

Now and then Kurt gathered his disciples around for a day of games with him and his theories. On one of those afternoons, I heard the sound of the abyss surrounding us.

I sat in a corner. Kurt and his flock — they came from everywhere — sat in a circle in the middle of the room. If we talked, prayed, and meditated long enough, he told us, the group would break out in a hosanna of *insight* that held the seed of the Spirit. And so they talked and talked and exclaimed and watched Kurt for his approval. The more I listened, the farther I retreated into my corner. I felt like a toad who smelled a killer viper in the weeds.

Into my solitude, like a snapped twig, Kurt spoke to me: "Ned, we must hear from you now." The demon stutter that came to torment me every now and then slithered up my throat. I spoke, but as I did (I do not remember what I said), I heard a whirring sound somewhere in the room, and when I walked back to the corner I saw under a table a tape recorder that had taken down all I said on a shining brown wire.

We returned after dinner to listen to the recording of the whole afternoon. When I heard my voice, it licked through the cold room, the two-headed monster of my stammer pouring like tar through my throat. I fainted.

The center crumbled. The house fell into a silent, rasping anger.

Michael Green, who had visited the center on the days Kurt had his revels, warned me that Kurt was in extremis; sooner or later there'd be trouble. I decided to escape; I would hitchhike with Michael to Notre Dame for a summer school session in liturgical studies.

The end came fast. David spoke to no one. Mary vanished into her room, climbed into bed, and refused to move. She asked me to go out and buy her silk stockings. I brought food to her bedside, where she lay like a child with nightmares and sexual mumps under an enormous pile of blankets.

The day before Green and I left for Notre Dame, David and I made a trip to Coalville, a wretched little town heaving its last breath in the drafts of coal refineries and stripped hills. The town appeared demented that day. Every woman seemed to wear coils of hair curlers in her hair; the men seemed yellow and crumpled with the burden of their life in the mines, as if clear air were an alien element they breathed with disgust, preferring the closed shafts of the mines to any light, to life. The stores were piled high with junk: toothpaste, paper plates, plastic toys, and cheap clothes. It was a city of ugly forms, lost desires, and death. It mirrored the center: debris, debris, debris.

Kurt stormed through the house in a fit of panic as he watched his dream destroyed. David wandered, flushed, red, and brooding, up and down the stairs. He took to the showers and stood under scalding water until I feared he'd dissolve. I remember him naked, staring across the bathroom at me, his eyes red from the heat, steam rising from his skin, his arms hard as the timber he carried up the hills of the farm covered with soap. I packed my suitcase and hid from Kurt. Mary pulled the covers over her head, and in the middle of the night I got up and sneaked away.

8

Hopeless Hall

I RETURNED TO BRADFORD FOR THE SUMMER IN 1955. I had graduated from St. Michael's in 1953. Father had taken his leave from us into his secret life, and there was nothing we or he could do about it. He made a quick visit. We fought. He vanquished. We wept. When we shut the house down in September, we never returned to it again.

Hopeless Hall was gathered like a pile of brown Victorian mantelpieces into one vast building on the edge of a tainted, dour lake. The water seemed to have seeped into it from rotted tree trunks felled in a forest fire that lay half burned and moldering on the shore. Air and light rattled around six stories of cracked plastered walls and found no congenial forms to touch, no places to set alive with their beneficence. My rooms were on the fifth floor: two long, narrow, cell-like boxes painted a streaked yellow. In the study were a rolltop desk, two chairs, a rocker, and a couch with a spring shooting out through a cushion. Past a door hung with plastic shower curtains, my bedroom: a cot, a chest, a black-shaded high window. The smell of long-locked-up clothes. In the lower part of the door that led into the hall was a crack a foot long and wide enough to let light in. Freshly made splinters lay on the floor, as if an ax had been laid to the door minutes before. The view from the window onto the lake and over the burned forest and trees to a field of stunted brush and rocks was blurred and oily through the grimy glass.

I thought of professors walking with hands behind their backs toward oak-paneled drawing rooms for sherry. Behind them boys: mannered, blue-jacketed, smiling, talking of kites, football, and girls. I saw wives of professors lifting teapots, looking out on lawns of daffodils and singing birds. I heard, in my dreams of academe, bells calling children to dinner, and in the dining room I saw blazing chandeliers reflected in polished oak tables.

On the night of my arrival, the dean invited me to supper. I was praised for taking on the job; teachers were hard to find, and though Hopeless Hall may not yet have been the finest school in the East, it was making its way proudly. (I had expected silver and china, fireplaces and linen, but it was all overstuffed furniture and five-and-dime dishes.) The dean hinted that something had gone wrong in the school during the month preceding my hiring. He did not easily tell me what it was; someone had been discovered in an ungentle-manly act — someone had seriously risked the school's reputation. I pressed him, and, blushing and turning his eyes away, he said that my predecessor had been found in bed with one of the boys. The boy remained; the teacher was sent away during the night.

It was hard for me to understand just what had happened, but I went to my rooms less enchanted than I wished to be on my first night in a *school.*

I served one weekend a month as a hall proctor. Until then I had lived a private life, and I found barging into strange rooms and crowded bathrooms unpleasant. I had no idea how to order anyone to do anything. The boys — no stylish lads from the social register — were a slimy lot of near-delinquents. The dean told me to listen outside doors for trouble and to surprise the students in the bathroom now and then to keep them on their guard. But I couldn't do such underground work, and the boys quickly discovered I couldn't and raised hell freely from the first day they saw me.

My English classes were gentle, nervous, hectic disasters. I taught well, I think, with love and with delight in the act of teaching. I looked young; I was a couple of years older than the oldest of my students. I was as innocent as the most experienced, and experienced as the most innocent. My pedagogy rocketed from me with grand gestures that I hoped would keep my classes quiet. I stammered; it returned on occasion; they giggled. I tricked them into submission on the first day by reading aloud to them Poe's "Masque of the Red Death." Only my love for the texts I chose held us together. I made them buy *The Iliad* and *The Odyssey,* and it riveted them to their seats. I clobbered them with Melville, Henry James, and Shakespeare, and cared not a whit whether or not they understood. It was perhaps the best class I ever taught. Even that crew, immersed so suddenly into such wonder, could not help but rise to it, and sometimes they smiled when we hit a stride and forgot our troubles. They found me a snob. I found them vulgarians. We hated each other; we loved each other. We fought. We shouted. We stormed. They laughed. But when we spoke of poetry and of certain men — Aeneas, Ulysses, Melville's crew — we came together and listened.

I could not bear the faculty. The atmosphere of male teachers and male students stank of virginity — not physical virginity, but the dirty-sock, unwashed-shirt, shaving-cream virginity of single men and boys living together in rooms unlit by women and flowers. Sex was everywhere, grunting and squealing. Two of my students held hands across the aisle when they knew I was looking in their direction, and one day unzipped their trousers and put their hands into their underwear and pulled out their erect penises. The class watched to see what I would do. I told them to leave the room, and they did with their arms around each other, their tongues stuck out at me. The class roared with laughter. I went on talking about Emily Dickinson.

The boys were the children of the nouveau riche: hairdressers, undertakers, the quick-war rich, and a lump of sons of deposed South American dictators. The Irish Catholic headmaster was a retired admiral. He had the manner of a sadomasochistic floorwalker. To the parents, he was *class*. He wielded with swaggering arrogance a deference to the parents that appalled my sense of style. He had no habit more curious and frightening than his light step, contrived as a piece of lace on a riding boot. He ought to have lumbered and stumbled, but he floated, skimmed the surface of the floor, mingling fragility and hardness, but without grace — like a hyena. He curled his lips in a pink-gummed grin and spoke in fitful oily seriousness that exposed nothing as brutally as the stupidity he would conceal.

My students mocked me and laughed at me and would have driven me out, but my youth saved me. One boy stalked me through the corridors, stood silently outside my door, lurked in the bathroom when I shaved, climbed a tree and looked down on me when I read on the lawn. He popped out of corners and stood so close to me I could feel his breath on my face. He walked up to me once, took the glasses from my face, and crushed them beneath his foot. I grabbed him and shook him, and he took me into his arms and kissed me on the mouth. I hit him in the stomach and sent him howling down the hall. The headmaster did nothing. His father was rich, and Hopeless Hall loved nothing so much as a rich boy in extremis.

I had been writing every day to Dorothy Van Ghent, the great American critic and friend from my college days in Vermont, at St. Michael's, and David, the ex-monk from the Community of Christ the Redeemer. They kept me sane. Poems came up like crocuses through the darkness. When the boys whooped it up down the halls and threw empty Coke bottles up toward the ceiling so that they crashed outside my door, when they peed over the stairwell, when they flooded the bathrooms, even when two of them stood on their beds when I came into their room to stop a fight and began to masturbate, I still ground out poems. (I could not write for a week when I found a glob of spit floating on the surface of my soup like a scab.) My first poems were humorous incantations about the glory of life and the predicament of manhood bowling over the child. I had trouble with the last line of the third stanza of a poem in a wild, disjointed series of lyrics. I sent it to Dorothy:

> I am a dull mosaic boy
> Byzantine and fluid-eyed
> fey collapsed with falling down
> the passages along the sun.
>
> Wide-eyed and crazed, procession wise,
> accustomed to the length of days
> when princes stood along the wall
> astounded and amazed.
>
> Numb and dazzled, drenched in gold
> from head to toe I'm struck,
> becoming slowly like a rose
> in tesserae of gold bedazed.
>
> This dark comparison I hold
> above me, high and still,

stuns music into ambergris,
myself to accomplished loveliness.

And in this, the very start of youth,
remarkable seems the day,
for I am dull, mosaic, masked,
with head of rose, in thunder cast.

The fourth line in the third stanza had read:

to vanish like a rose when told.

Dorothy put her foot down in two letters:

The "dull mosaic boy": I quite like this one — it's very
engaging — but I have a feeling it could be worked on
a little for perfection.

I struggled and wrote a new line, and Dorothy
approved:

First the mosaic boy. Yes Yes Yes you really have it
now! The lines
    Becoming slowly like a rose —
    in tesserae of gold bedazed.
are *Just Perfect!* (This is one of those astonishing things
that sometimes happens on a forced re-writing. One
inevitably resents and suspects the alien push to alter-
ation; and then under-the-pressure something wonderful happens.) I also like the last line. The poem is *truly
wholly made* now. I am so pleased.

About the literary life she had a regal contempt:

> I went to a party the other evening at Philip Rahv's in
> Boston — just Cal Lowell and his wife were there.
> Gosh it was so literary I felt utterly illiterate. I didn't
> know half the things they were talking about. After-
> wards I had a dream about Rahv. He asked me what
> was the difference between nomans and drivens in
> Kafka. They both looked to me like foam rubber ash-
> trays — the nomans gray and the drivens tan. He said I
> should look them up in the Boston Public Library or
> the Catholic Encyclopedia. I said, "But I'm not really a
> literary person." He said, "So I see. I am."

Dorothy gave the sign when to send my poems off
to a magazine. "They are ready now," she wrote, and I
mailed nearly half my first book to *Botteghe Oscure*,
typed on heavy bond paper. I waited for weeks, for
years, expecting a Roman stamp on an envelope and a
note from Princess Caetani taking the whole bunch. I
visited *Botteghe Oscure* years later looking for them, as a
father would for lost children. No one knew anything
about them.

David wrote me a letter a day. His love for me did
not curb his rage at my priggish intellectual vanity.
When I complained that my students didn't understand me, he wrote:

> You must try to live-with your aversion — keen though
> it be — to currying the mangy little-steeds-who stable in
> the paddock at the Hall. Kids are cowed by the thought

of "teacher —" altogether apart from O'Gorman either O'Gorman now or O'Gorman later. To the student-the English teacher is a skeleton-having-odd-pounds-of-flesh-and-paid-to-terrorize-the-class-with-Preposition-that-Govern-the-Dative.

Teaching is partly then (for you-) a business of English; it is partly a question of managing whatever little genius there happens to exist within yourself; it is partly a question of outguessing the more stupid.

To be succinct; no high school lads or girls at Hopeless Hall or elsewhere are prepared for a seminar on either theodicy or fish: undeceive yourself on that point. Let me be even bitterer: furthermore, I think that you have probably flunked too many. Try to get this: Today the high school teacher (notice I said to-day — things should be quite different) is a mere bailiff hired to entertain the kids while they are not on the street. I don't expect you to agree; and too-I don't know Hopeless Hall. I am however raising my eye-brows at the news that you have done thus and so. Quit talking rank Scholasticism to even the brightest and keep your flunking to a minimum.

You must try to inhabit many mansions — and to inhabit them successfully — inhabit them with a purpose. Poetry will serve you but ill until you are a better poet.

You must try to live in bread and butter consciousness.

Milton has strange power. Promethean dionysiac *et alii*. For the rest smoke a little and remember perhaps *le Corps Mystique* — if that is not fractured French.

Hunger weariness and humiliation are great teachers. Which of them dwells with you these days.

God is the common denominator who bridges all the gaps I suspect. The worst is yet to come perhaps. However even to know this fact is to be "prepared."

Events, like morning glories, tend to overwhelm the most thought-out order, and on a Saturday night when I was doing my turn as proctor, they did.

At nine, I had settled down to correct papers. In the hall, the boys were setting up a bowling alley: a wedge of bottles and empty cans at the end of the sloping, buckling floor. They rolled basketballs down the hall, letting out great shrieks of pleasure when they made a strike. When the noise of bouncing cans and broken bottles got damnable enough to get me up from my seat, I went to the door and told them to stop. "Up your ass," they shouted as a basketball shot past me. I closed the door and tried to get back to work. By then I didn't give a damn what my students did, though I did rough up a fellow who hid himself in a dark corner near a confessional and sent around loud announcements of his fellow students' sins. The noise, however, trebled. A bunch of them came outside my door and urinated under it, flooding my room with piss. I opened the door and said I'd cancel all their weekends if they did not shut up and return to their rooms. They moved in on me. I told them that they'd get me down eventually, but not until a couple got tossed over the banister — they'd maneuvered me there when I tried to get away. They got directly in front of me, and a stockbroker's son touched the point of a knife he pulled from his trousers to my groin. I lifted up my hand to strike him in the throat, but suddenly they scattered, giving me a wide berth when they passed. I stood like an angel of destruction in their bowling alley.

The mother of the headmaster had watched the whole thing from the door of her room at a cloistered end of the hall. She had a fancy for me, and she toddled up to me in her filthy and threadbare cotton nightshirt with a glass of whisky on a tray. She ran her hand down my cheek, winked, and waddled away — eighty-five years old — her rosary flapping from her hand like a dry weed.

In the middle of the night, a bottle flew through the transom. They tried to break down my door, and I did nothing but lie quietly waiting. The door stood firm, the crack in it still unrepaired, a relict from the night they had found a teacher in bed with one of their pals.

The term was nearly over. I corrected examinations and told the admiral I was leaving. He looked at me with his mindless cordiality — face like the barrel of a gun — shook my hand, saluted, gave me a check and a cup with Hopeless Hall's crest emblazoned on it like a scar, and called for a car to take me to the train.

I landed in New York, cast up like a wreck in my mother's apartment, where she had moved after my father left us to go work in Boston at a detective agency. It was Christmas, and our Airedale, Peggy, had been shipped to the city to spend the holidays. She arrived in an enormous wooden cage burdened with melan-

choly and sat curled up through the festivities in a corner, where she received our homage. On the day after
New Year's, we put her back in her wooden cage and
had her shipped back to Boston, where Father inhabited his secret world.

In the spring term of 1955, I started graduate school at
Columbia. I rented a room in a redbrick building on
the corner of Hudson and Perry Streets, whose two
windows looked down over the traffic, a view I loved,
for I saw trucks, workmen, children, drunkards, and
dockmen going to and from work, school, and the mil-
lion bars that in those years gave the streets a lusty village kind of life. It was the first room I had ever rented.
In a corner, a yellow-stained sink; and, scattered like
junk from an abandoned attic, a sinking bed, a red
table, a wicker chair, and a chest. Roaches and built-in
smells. But I thought it was a castle. The first poem I
wrote in it, I wrote at one sitting a few months after I
had begun my classes at Columbia:

> The rose and the body of the rose
> the stem the balustrade of air
> the pith of darkness in the fist
> the rose and body of the rose.
>
> The wolf and body of the wolf
> the jaw and the marrow in the skull
> the furnace fastened in the eye
> the wolf and the body of the wolf.

The wren and the body of the wren
the wing and the vessel of its flight
the lyre and its rustic throat
the wren and the body of the wren.

The shark and the body of the shark
the sudden mouth and fix of knife
the panic shackled to the fin
the shark and the body of the shark.

The snake and the body of the snake
the twist of choking in the grass
the feet of scorpion on the tongue
the snake and the body of the snake.

The bat and the body of the bat
the flash of demi bird and slap
the divination of the chin
the bat and the body of the bat.

No one ever saw the inside of my room. Mike
Harrington lived in the room next door. His life was
mysterious and well connected: he knew John Cogley,
Robert Hutchins; he had studied at Yale and was vice
president of the Young People's Socialist League. We
complimented each other on the filth of our rooms. I
never saw the inside of his room, nor he mine. (We ad-
mitted with alarming vigor one night that we had not
changed our pillowcases in a month.)

I was given Aunt Yvette's old curtains — red
background, yellow-orange flowers — and walked up
Bleecker Street with them past stalls of fresh vegeta-

bles, past nuns and mothers pushing carriages — past the people in their freedom. I thought I was handsome, a poet; life was everywhere, and every inch of me fed on it.

I found myself by accident in the seventeenth century. Graduate students must have their century. Scholarship, graduate seminars, bright-eyed, solemn professors, and especially a terrifying class on the origins of English harangued me with tasks of the intellect I knew I'd fail. I'd never thought very much about study; I failed courses in English and history because till now I had been lazy and simply uninterested in grades and lectures. But at Columbia I had to work. I decided to write my thesis on *The Faerie Queene:* "Sir Guyon as Anti-Hero," I grandly called it. I was delighted with the title: elegant, unworldly, pretentious . . . and meaningless. I loved the poem, but as it droned on, I thought I'd go mad, for when Spenser is a bore, there is no greater bore in literature; when he is not a bore, when he sings, he is the grandest of poets. I had a desk wedged in between bookshelves in a sub-basement of Butler Library. I was deadly earnest. I read everything, made notes, and thought I'd uncovered the very brain of literature. I wrote a thesis that I am terrified someone might someday read. I look now and then at a copy, and it is absolutely unreadable. It is a game of a poet playing around, like a child with jacks, with ideas and symbols that he knows nothing about; except, of course, that they are ideas and symbols and have a life of their own outside his understanding. I learned a good deal reading that poem. It was a blind journey into wonderful music, and I was blessed by what I heard.

The professors were paragons of dandyesque intellectual bearing. Lionel Trilling wielded his Jewish
critical-angular perceptions like a whip, clipping speculation and grinding his classes to frozen attention. His
voice broke like pebbles and sand over his desk. There
was something irretrievable in his insights, as if once
he had spoken, the doors of speculation were slid shut,
bolts rumbled into place, and the subject was closed.

Jacques Barzun was a natty boulevardier who
knew thousands of dates and parked himself on knowledge, crossed his legs, tapped the gold-tipped case of
his wit, and barraged me with irony, mock cynicism,
paradox, and a veiled interior lamentation on the state
of the world. Eric Bentley seemed privy to all knowledge and disdainful of common birds; I perched like a
crow on the cactus of his perceptions, and when I dared
to speak, he took my thought and tore into it as if it
were a hive of hornets and he the avenging flame-
thrower. He fixed an idea with his energy rapid-fire,
concentrated seamlessly, and built an edifice of can-
tilevered and hot-limbed reason that soared and always
hit the mark. In the reaches of Hamilton Hall, Marjorie
Nicholson reigned and taught, chairman of the Graduate School, conducting her classes like the interiors of
clocks and space machines. All she did and said was a
masterwork of precision and force, scholarship and in-
tuitive design. She had her lectures under such control
that when she spoke the final word of her lecture for
the day, the bell for the end of class rang.

The man I wanted to see was Mark Van Doren, for

it was known that he possessed Olympian powers and was supposed to have — as well — a heart.

I'd no notion what such a man would be like — brilliant cold heart, very old, and ready to blow away blunderers like me. When he walked into the room the first time to talk about "great books," he came in un-Olympian, loose, stepped up without fanfare to a long raised platform, opened a notebook, and thought aloud about Virgil. He spoke as if it were not indecorous to love poetry; as if he loved it. He taught like a strolling player. He visited his classes the way a balladeer might visit a village. When he spoke of Homer, Virgil, Dante, Cervantes, Shakespeare, Ariosto, Molière, he blessed them with a rich flowering delight that came not just from him but from his students' entrance into them. He opened our minds as he opened the text; at the same time effortlessly, no heavy leap from text to explication, to the mind of his class. We waited on Van Doren's words like runners on the starting gun. He never spoke of Virgil, for instance, as if he were better than we, and he never spoke to us as if we were less than he. I used to think, "So that's the meaning, is it? So that's the trick of the poem, that's the form, the style." But it came from us, not from Mark. It did, of course, come from him, but he made it seem as if it came from us, and that was the secret of his teaching.

I gathered my poems and brought them to his office. I paced up and down outside his door, made a few false starts to leave, knocked, walked in, put them on his desk, asked him to read them, said I'd be back in a

week, and got out as fast as I could. I'd given my lambs
and sheep to the dragon, and if he devoured them, it
would serve me right for yielding them up to such a famous dragon. I awaited the ax. My lambs lay there,
white throats neatly spread back for the kill. But Mark
smiled and said he loved my poems, thought them
beautiful, mentioned Shakespeare when he told me of
their excellence. My God, I thought, Van Doren the
Olympian *likes* these things! I floated across the campus.

Each poem I wrote I brought to him. That first
poem I wrote, I dedicated to Mark Van Doren, who
wrote back, almost immediately: "I am pleased and
proud of your poem, which shows you leaning out of
heaven's window on Hudson Street and seeing everything in sight." He never refused them; he read them,
usually thought well of them, though he never lacked
the time to tell me how dumb my guardianship of the
muse often was. I said, when he asked me what a poem
meant, "Oh, it could mean this or it could mean that."
"No," he said, "it cannot mean this or that. It must
mean one thing." He did not mean "one thing" the
way a piece of apple is merely a piece of apple; he
meant it the way a man speaks of a seamless cloth: one
thing; one life; one trajectory, no matter how various it
might be in intention.

Amid the tweed acid flounce and jabot airs of Columbia, he was a serpent among doves and a dove
among serpents. He was a canny detachment in a world
of mostly men whose *Congressional Report* and Holy
Writ is the *Modern Language Journal*. He suggested I
take my poems to a publisher. I thought about it for

weeks and then, dressed in T-shirt, khakis, and sneakers, I brought an envelope sealed with Scotch tape to Harcourt Brace. I asked the receptionist — in a whisper — for the poetry editor. "Yes," she said, loud and clear, "I'll call her. Sit down, please." There were others in the room, and I thought they looked at me, sneering: "A poet. Fine thing. Look at his shoes. No tie." I felt as if my stutter were waiting to blast me again. A lady came out, introducing herself as Margaret Marshall. She took the envelope, thanked me, and vanished.

I thought it was all very final.

On Christmas Day, 1954, shortly before I started at Columbia, wrapped to the nose in an eight-foot bright red scarf, I had visited the Catholic Worker in its old house on Chrystie Street in the middle of the Bowery. I had heard of it all my days in college as the place where Dorothy Day, judge, saint, and revolutionary, gave food, clothing, hope, and fellowship to the poor and bedeviled. I was searching still for some coign in the world where I'd find poetry, life, the Church, and man.

I walked up the steps to the front door, knocked, and when no one answered, entered a large, warm room, rumbling with the people of the streets. There was disarray there, some smell I couldn't name, and a carelessness and simplicity I'd never known before. The roaches and flies that loped through the dust seemed not all malevolent. It was a place of no illusions.

A beautiful girl was mopping up a pool of vomit. I

offered to help her. She wouldn't give up the mop. It was Eileen, the girl I came close to marrying.

I looked at the poor then as a sort of superhumanity, wistful nomads who had burned away all their defects and moved through despair, soft, dumb, and immaculate. I felt very rich amid that poverty. What better thing to do, I thought, than take off my jacket, wallet in pocket, change in pocket, and hang it over a chair. An offering. The mopping girl watched me, set her mop against the wall, and locked my coat away. "You know," she said, "they'll steal it. If you want to help, go downstairs and ask Smokey Joe what to do."

Smokey Joe was a mammoth wreck, a marvel of holiness and ruined humor. His conversation of the road and alleyways was murky but ornate with the brutalities and wisdom of the Bowery. He never aged. His face vanished into lines and tormented grimaces, but he drove on through life with the energy of an olive tree gripping the world with gnarled ferocity. He did not welcome me to his domain. "Wait until I call you," he said. The men of the Bowery had lined up down the block, waiting for their soup and meat. They came in a few at a time to fill up the empty places at long wooden tables, huddled in their rags like moles in a sunless crevice, starved horses. No beauty in them to me. I was afraid to touch them; they smelled of piss and cursed the world, and when they passed, I held my breath.

The Catholic Worker is the domain of men and women who have no world but the Bowery, where they hide, awaiting death. Dorothy Day and her workers fed them, clothed them, and gave them a place to sit and talk as they awaited their fate.

Dorothy, like all great men and women, was a peasant. She dressed and walked like a woman ready to go into the fields to pick the fruit of the harvest, to wash linen in a stream, or to teach a child about the transformation of a cocoon to a butterfly; and like a peasant, too, she had the breeding of a queen in her manner. She spoke of the dispossessed of Christ and the world with fearless and simple charity. She cut away with a scythe of honesty and compassion any illusions Christians might have about the extent of their responsibility in a world of starvation and plenty. The usual image of the revolutionary is that of a hard-bitten, striding hoyden bellowing through her corsets of tumult and the blowing up of cities. But Dorothy's text of revolution is the Gospel, and she fed the hungry, clothed the naked, visited the sick, and built places for the lost to rest.

The church at the Worker was then unbuttoned. In the center of the blasted world of the Bowery, she was poor, nomadic, suffering, perilous, and weak. And because she was so fragile, the spirit seemed to sing there especially loudly.

On Friday night at the Worker, a speaker would be invited to talk to the wild men of the Bowery. They would shoot him down afterward with questions that were often explications of the texts of their lives. "Why," asked Mary Mother of God (the nickname of a bundle of ragged deranged womanhood), "do you advocate sexual relationships between nuns and priests?" I had spoken about Dante, but I tried to answer, for she questioned me from the rationale of her derangement, and I revered such anguish.

Afterward, my comrades at the Worker and I would troop off to the White Horse on Hudson Street for a night of beer and metaphysics. (Dorothy disapproved of drinking; we feared she'd discover our bohemian ways.)

Mary Ann McCoy, Norman Stein, John Stanley, Anne Marie Stokes, Eileen Good, Agnes Bird, Betty Bartelme, Ed Egan, Elizabeth Richards, Frank Murphy, Michael Harrington, Eleanor Corrigan, Martin Corbin, and Rita Ham took over the back room of the Horse and shouted out loud about sex, God, revolution, history, poetry, the Church, faith, life, and the wonderful moment in time when we were all together — so brilliant and so wise.

Each of us had his vocabulary, a particular way of dressing, and a moral hat we wore, always at the same angle. Isaac spoke of his sexual exploits with lamenting agony and gutter vulgarity that fooled no one into thinking he was ever as impure as he wished to be. He said again and again to every girl he saw, "I'd like to fuck you if you're a virgin." Ed Egan sang Mozart and Irish folk songs in a hapless, edgy tenor voice: he sang as his motto "La Ci Darem la Mano," from *Don Giovanni*, and the drunker he got, the louder he sang, and the more we loved him. Ed Murphy read the most arcane of books and was famous for his knowledge; Anne Marie Stokes had been in the French Resistance during the war and had spent an air raid under a table with Paul Valéry. John Stanley was an ex-monk, exotically gentle, who cooked great feasts in his apartment, where we gathered like hermits to drink wine and listen to Gregorian chants in candlelight. Betty Bartelme, Agnes Bird, and Eleanor Corrigan hovered about us all with chaste, hot, mortal femininity.

We tried to brush the edges of blasphemy, and I recall with special gusto one Good Friday night when we all got very drunk and walked home early in the morning, wicked and happy. The next evening we swarmed into the White Horse, an unheard-of thing for the more orthodox of us to do. Holy Saturday was a sacred day, when one did nothing. A pack of Communists and socialists, tattered and dour, mocked our piety and sang revolutionary songs; we countered with hymns and chant. That evening Bill Clancy — an editor of *Commonweal* — walked into the back room of the White Horse, rejoicing like a child who had come upon a treasure in a garden for just an hour before, he told us, he had received the Eucharist at mass, with all the church singing the Pange Lingua, as he walked up the aisle to his seat, the host still on his tongue. Early in the morning when the sun was rising, Eileen, Mary Ann, Ed Egan, and I blustered into the San Remo Bar on McDougal Street and sang the Salve Regina. After each stanza, we crashed an empty glass on the floor. The manager threw us out, and I beat it down the street, Eileen running after me, calling me to return and talk to her. She caught up with me and grabbed my scarf, which was flying in the cold early spring dawn. I felt it spin off my neck, and when I turned to see if I were free from her, I saw her standing in the rain with my scarf in her hand. In a little storm that whipped up out of the Easter sky, I walked back alone to my room.

Eileen was Italian, her family from Turin and Florence. I think of her as Florentine, full of compassion and suffering, but love played second fiddle to my ego's dreams, and I looked at her one day and said, "My heart is made of ice." She did not say it wasn't, or if she did, I knew she was wrong.

She had set up housekeeping in Puerto Rican Harlem with Mary Ann McCoy. They decided to live there to give themselves and their love to the poor. The children who wandered there in a wilderness of rats, crime, vice, and the perverse dominion of the city came to her door for consolation, humor, and food. I would go there after a day bent over *The Faerie Queene*, and she would rub my back with alcohol as I lay on her bed drinking red wine and munching on a pizza.

They were blessed days. I wrote my first review for *Commonweal* — of Marianne Moore's *Predilections*. When he appeared one day at the White Horse, Mike Harrington told me gloatingly he had bought all of the novels of Dickens for five dollars! We had been talking, too, about a Marxist interpretation of the Book of Kings.

Soon the tribe began to disappear into the strange places of their lives, far from the cloisters of the Worker and the White Horse. One, in a fit of sorrow, drank a bottle of Lysol. A girl we all loved showed us some pictures of two naked Yale freshmen and threw herself later that night in front of a car. One fell from our radical grasp and became an editor of the *National Review*.

All of us wandered in a dark and lonely place, where we had to find our own style and make accommodations to the world.

I was turning into a drifter. It was time too for me to learn the craft of poetry. Dorothy Van Ghent wrote me,

> I wish you had money to go to Kenyon and write for a year under Ransom. For continuity into the years ahead I don't feel you have yet in your bloodstream the sense of form that makes for continuity of effort and achievement for renewal in the arteries of tradition. With Ransom you'd probably be all irritation at first — although it might be just the opposite, it might seem like coming "home" for he has in the literary way (and in the non-Roman philosophical way the pagan philosophical way) the masculine breeding in the sense of time and history and form and meaning and the beauty of these when they are perceived formally — what is part of your own deep attraction for the Church. Also, of course, he has personally the beauty and detachment of courtesy — the spreading laurel tree — and I understand that anyone who associates with him experiencing that sweet Socratic green shade becomes the same way if he isn't that way already. (And you are.)

My first literary journey was a trek to Dartmouth College to read my poems before the Thursday poets. I practiced in front of a mirror for days; walked in the woods, bellowing them to the sky, my voice booming out to the void. I sounded like a bard, I thought; all I needed to do was to carry my vanity up the stairs in the library to my audience. I dreaded the return of the Stammer Demon. I opened my mouth and knew I was done for. I stepped on the scorching gridiron of my demon. I wanted to run but found myself rooted to the rug, inflicting on my body and my soul the demon's scratching, howling claws. My tongue stuck, and the poems came out blasted, fractured, distended like entrails. Shaking with shame and anger, I ran out into a blizzard.

I limped back to the city filled with thoughts of death and the halt promise of possession by the Stammer Demon. But soon all was gracious and sweet again, for I fell in with Ivan Illich, the dissident Catholic priest who founded a center for radical Catholic political activists in Cuernavaca, Dorothy Day, Anne Fremantle, a salonist frequented by Evelyn Waugh, Elizabeth Bowen, Auden, Shirley Hazzard, Jim Kritzeck, a professor at Princeton who was knighted by the pope for delivering converts out of Egypt when they were in danger of imprisonment, and Helen Iswolsky, the daughter of the last czarist ambassador to Paris and an intellect of great vigor. We met in the back room of Liz Sullivan's bookstore and tried to unearth the church. I loved theology and Illich. A young, restive, cryptic, mournful, eagle-limbed priest was our teacher, to whom theology was a sensuous rich bread. He taught me to taste it and to settle for nothing less than its gentle luxuriant storms and biases.

In the spring I got, the way frozen fields in Bradford got crocuses, a Guggenheim Fellowship. I had no thoughts from then on but wild and burning ones of Europe. Trilling recited a poem to me, when I told him of my good luck on the steps of Hamilton Hall:

> It is no longer a forlorn hope
> That I shall be in Ethiope.

In Bradford Academy I had covered margins of books, the top of my desk, and my missal with the emblem when I was a boy of the unattainable — Roma Roma Roma. Piranesi prints hung on my classroom walls; what brambled arcane worlds they are! I wonder often how much I owe Piranesi and the *National Geographic* for the rhythms of my poetry. I ran my finger over the map of Europe, down the west coast of Ireland to Clare, my father's land, and then to the shores of Brittany, where Mother's family began their wars with time. I imagined myself walking up to ancient doors and finding, twined among ivy and wild flowers, the crest of my blood hammered into salt-blasted, carved, and primitive walls and archways of ruined castles. But Rome was the pith, the heart, the center of my dreams.

In August 1956, the *Andrea Doria* sank off the coast of Cape Cod. I walked along the beach looking for signs of the wreck: a cask of jewels, a corpse, a piece of hull. I sailed for England the eighth of September. The whistle blew, and the ship moved away from the dock like a continent slipping away from the boundaries of the land.

9

Europe

*E*UROPE, 1956: MY FIRST JOURNEY AWAY FROM NEW England, an itinerary that included London, Dublin, Turkey, Greece, Naples, Florence, Venice, Paris, and Rome.

I lost myself in London's fog, reveled in Naples. Rome rescued me from frivolity. I know no one there. I have no ease with the language. Yet it is the only place on earth where I do not feel like a man in exile. My son's ashes lie under a tree in the Vatican Gardens. I was first in love there, and was broken by that love. It was a delirium, and in Rome delirium is banished. I have languished there in sadness, but when I saw what was about me, the sadness could not impose its sanctions.

So I have written about that place, so filled with life, but distant, cruel, restive, with an everlasting splendor. It is as I remember it. It is now the same. It does not change. It increases. It is a city without margins, boundaries, gates. It cannot but welcome eternity.

I could not have been dazzled more by my cabin on the *Liberté* had it been lined with watered silk and hung with precious tapestries. Pipes and wires crisscrossed the ceiling and down the walls. It had no window and no bath. A board across the sink served me as a desk. I sat at it like Byron settling down to attend to his vision. I went to sleep late that first night out, pacing the deck until the ship had entered the open sea. I got up at dawn to look at the sun rising over the waves. The sea lay all about me, every point in the universe equidistant from the place I stood. I was the center. The waters moved me. They moved the ship; fired the furnaces in the hull. They were embedded in the magnets in the pilot's compass, and they drove me, sure as a hammer drives a nail into a wall, to the land I sailed toward. I wrote to my mother about those first days on the sea:

> We are out now three days and strange days they have been. Life on a ship is full of dull excitement. The sea is always grand and fearsome. I love the long days. I sit and read and sleep. It is timeless, the sea, and I have lost the feeling of time. I love the isolation of the sea and I search out no one but sit in one place and wait for porpoises, whales, and albatross. I think the most splendid thing about the Atlantic is that each day is the same but in its mystery and vastness holds variety with cataclysmic aplomb. I remembered the turtle, ageless

and vicious, that is rumored to crawl around the bottom of Lake Morey.

The sea was the net that caught each tremor and shift of light, every sensuous blind-fall, each desire of my flesh and of my imagination. I sat on the deck, far from other passengers, in rain and sun, wrapped in blankets, on my deck chair, heart enchained to every shift and bucking of the surface. The sea is mask and naked form. It is the force that hides, exposes, settles down the imagination, and then shatters it. It seems to come fresh from the hand of God. There is no mind in the sea, only the sheer possibility of power. The sea's brainless energies were an affront to Eros. Often I wished for the torrid land when the sea's gray perfection tore light and peace from my eyes. I dreamed one night of the gardens and lawns of Southport and of the sound in the distance, benevolent and simple. Each thrust forward of the bow was a rampage over Poseidon's countryside. I delighted to think of what that landscape was, which soared on like devastation's triumph under the keel.

Gulls, in their messenger growl, hovered about the stern as we neared land. There was a cruel force in their eyes as they swooped down from the sky and glided about the ship, always a distance off, as if the boat were harbinger of attack and they were the sullen scouts of the enemy. I waited for land with delicious anxiety. The sea had overtaken me. Each breath I took, each step, shuddered with the sea. My nerves had gotten a little drunk, for the sea was mistress of my farm-boy sensibil-

My mother, Annette de
Bouthillier-Chavigny O'Gorman,
and myself in 1931, when I
was two.

With my father, Samuel Franklin Engs O'Gorman, and
my sister Annette in Danbury. We owned a house
there to stable Father's horse, Leigh-Ho.

With Father and my sister
Patricia in Far Rockaway
in 1947.

Sitting with my nanny,
Lydia Hoffman, Patricia,
and Annette.

I am seven years
old, on Leigh-Ho.
Father told me that
Leigh-Ho was a
direct descendant
of the legendary
racehorse
Man O'War.

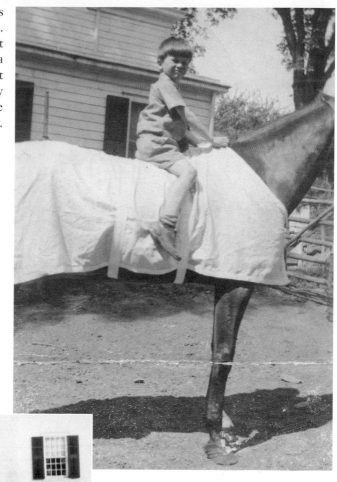

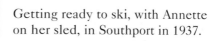

Getting ready to ski, with Annette
on her sled, in Southport in 1937.

In my confirmation best in Southport, 1939. My bedroom is on the top right.

Rick in Paris, 1978.

Father and son in 1994.

With David Leonard, a volunteer, and some of the children
from the school in 1970.

With Jerry, one
of my kids.

A clipping from the *Daily News*,
showing me with some of the kids
in the school's new location on
East 129th Street.

John Pedin/Daily News

Ned O'Gorman and kids settling in happily to their new Children's Storefront home on E. 129th St.

A child's garden of verses in Harlem

With some of the children, parents, teachers, and volunteers in front of
the new school, the Ricardo O'Gorman Garden, in 2004.

ities, and she demanded constant attention. And when the land did appear, it appeared suddenly, as if it had been hidden behind a wave, and it coasted up to the ship, surprising it with an alien dominion.

Suddenly, one morning, I saw the English country-side touch the horizon gently, with the precision of a cord on a bow tightening to admit the arrow. The land spilled out of the light, illumined like a leaf in early spring; the world shook from the sea: sky blue as a morning glory, cliffs white as the underside of the gulls' wings. A fleet of sailboats raced past the ship as it lumbered up Southampton Harbor. The ship had been brought low by the land, feeble as the power of the earth took over its freedom. The fields and little villages along the way glowed in the light, now no longer untrammeled as it was on the waters, but gathered in and tempered by the tangible horizon. The air seemed bolted to the green brilliance of the countryside. The ship might have been tied all the while to the foundations of the land, gently pulled there by her beauty, rising now out of the sea, easily, simply, regally.

Before I disembarked, as the ship ambled up the harbor, I went to the prow and leapt in the air for joy, danced a little, like an idiot bear, on the deck. I used to love to stand there in a storm, face in the wind, rain, and fog, salt spray, and sudden bolts of sunlight falling over me like blossoms from a demonic tree. I wedged myself at the point of the prow, where the ship cleaves a path through the sea, and looked down at the anchor jammed into the gaping hole that grasped it through the journey as a sling holds a stone.

I could see far off on a hillside the shape of a white horse drawn over an entire field. It flashed past me again on the train ride into London. I thought it had been a concoction of my mind when I saw it from the ship, but when I saw it a second time, I knew it was real and an omen of wonder.

All I knew of Europe was not of the substance of history, nor was it tethered to fact. It was all in my mind: the land of absolute and bizarre otherness. When I landed in London, alone, with no friends, a spectacle of what every Englishman must have remembered Americans to be from their time there in the war, I might as well have landed in the Amazon in the midst of a puberty rite. I thought each car I passed was the carriage of a duke: London taxis seemed grand and funereal to me.

I was certain that the English despised Americans. My first night in London I could not get the courage to go into a restaurant and ask for food, certain that if I did, my accent would be instantly recognized, and I'd be laughed at and asked to leave. I dressed exactly in the style expected of Americans: khakis, tweed jacket, crew cut, striped tie, loafers. I was very tall and very thin and convulsed with terror at being in such a strange place.

My childhood had prepared me for nothing. I had learned nothing in my schooling that spoiled my breakneck cousinship to the world. I thought everyone innocent, nothing evil, the universe beyond the thin-lipped patience of New England so far "beyond me" that while I was in England, the thought of Rome seemed it might take me to the end of the world. I was trapped in my own excitement. I could not move. I had no one to talk to but the waitress in the hotel. I thought of leaving London, returning home, for the idea that I should go anywhere "else" was so fraught with terror that many nights I went home and lay down on my bed and wept. (My letters to T. S. Eliot, Edith Sitwell, and Stephen Spender had all gone unanswered.)

After three weeks of traveling in England, I tried the doors of the publishing house Faber and Faber. A lady told me that they could not help me find a good bar (what I had come in to ask about), but she would "pass me on" to the National Book League. The librarian there sent me to David Archer's bookshop on Greek Street, where I met poets, painters, sculptors, novelists, millionaires, photographers, teachers, travel agents, university wardens, famous husbands and their wives and famous wives and their husbands, and a good many childlike adults and adultlike children.

I spoke to W. S. Graham, but he was busy with beer. He asked me something about tradition in American poetry, a difficult way to begin a friendship, poetic or otherwise. I brushed by the turtleneck sweater of Colin Wilson in front of departing Dannie Abse and just missed by a hair George Barker and Stephen Spender. I had a hectic evening in an Indian restaurant with the playwright Michael Hastings and some strip-tease dancers who used a little room beside our table to change their clothes and to smoke between acts. I tried to talk with David Wright and G. S. Fraser and an Irishman, but no one talked to me.

I went to the bars; to the French bar where everyone was famous or, if they weren't, at least knew famous people and could *reach* them. I went to the Caves of France, where I met growling, howling, ferocious Scotsmen, Francis Bacon, blackmailers, whores, homosexuals, and teddy boys who seemed to be awaiting the firing squad. Everyone hated Americans and kept asking me again and again about cowboys (I had never seen one), Indians, wide-open places, gangsters, and my car (I didn't have one).

It seemed to me that I had either not spoken to the right people, spoken to the wrong people, or spoken to the right and wrong people about the wrong things, and exposed myself as an American poet with a seriousness complex.

One night in London, I was asked to come for drinks in the basement flat of a noble lady. They were talking away about Bertie (Lord Russell), Maggie (Maggie Teyte), Edith (Edith Sitwell), and Tom (T. S. Eliot). A man took a fancy to me and called me "dear boy" and "darling American." There was a bit of conversation I remember: "Does he manage at all with men or women?" a critic asked a *Times* correspondent just back from a revolution in Africa. "Oh, he's good with everything; he's a great tweed ass. Tweed jacket, tweed socks, tweed shoes, tweed cock."

I walked in the fog, lost in the most painful sorrow.

I took off one night down a dark alley and noticed, as I ambled deep in misery, ladies in the doorways and on the curbs, swinging plastic pocketbooks that shone in the fog like jellyfish. Some walked dogs. Most stood still, watching each man as he passed. A rather tubby one in a white cape stepped onto the sidewalk as I passed and called out to me, "Do you want to do it, duck? A fiver will get me all night." I bolted down the alley toward the lights of Piccadilly. Whores were nowhere in my understanding of the world. I thought they might come charging down on me like a herd of elephants. As I ran, they exploded in a high, mocking giggle.

The Thames water was a pasty brown. The wings of the swans on its banks were sullied with grime, and their necks, when they bent beneath the surface, came up dripping with oil and slime. The farther down toward Greenwich the river flowed, the more intricate and pastorally brutal it became. The dry docks and the machinery of the port were surreal. (Now the docks have gone, and restaurants and theaters, paths and bookstalls, museums and gardens, have replaced whatever was wondrous then.) The moist force of the sluggish river lay against the London sky. Foghorns, the knocking of ferries against landings and steamers against piers, the call of gulls, and the invasion of fog, like the bending over of birches loaded with spring snow, were signs of mystery and fear to my simple and passionate dreams of the world.

I lunged through life in London, expecting pomegranates and getting prunes. In America I was a minor sun, and around me praise, friendship, family, and streets revolved, assuring me peace and haven. But abroad I was nowhere, and no one really cared who I was or would be.

An Anglican priest, a friend of T. S. Eliot's at Oxford, had written Eliot asking him to let me come for a visit. When Eliot's secretary wrote me saying the poet would meet me in his office at Faber and Faber, I accounted it my first European miracle. I arrived two hours early and sat on a bench in Russell Square, thinking of a man who was Homer, Dante, Virgil, and Cervantes to me in that spring of my poetic wanderings.

At exactly four, I walked into the building, expecting to find — I do not know what — a sign perhaps, burning in the air, pointing to his office? He greeted me kindly and showed me to a chair in front of his desk. When he stood to welcome me, I thought he seemed as tall as the ceiling, with the shoulders and bulk of a quarterback. I sat down and could have counted the motes in the air, so perfect my attention, so astonished my nerves that I should be *there*.

I told him about my journey to Scotland, and how close I felt on the moors to prehistory and dreams. He agreed — or at any rate he seemed to understand what I meant — and said that I should keep a lookout for the little people who dwelt beneath the thorn trees in Ireland. We talked about wildflowers, New England, and sailing along the coast of Maine. (He was surprised that I had never been to Maine.) He told me the name of the first book he had reviewed, and I told him the name of the first one I had reviewed. His office became a holy place. There he was, the Wizard, the Poet, the Maker of Epics, and here was Ned, exchanging words with him. When I left, he invited me to visit him in the spring. I told all my bar chums in the Coach and Horse and knew they envied me.

Victoria Ocampo, the exquisite Argentinean lady of letters, brought me a copy of *The Waste Land* inscribed to her by Eliot, for she had had tea with him in his house and thought I'd treasure such a gift. I carried it with me wherever I went, carefully wedging it in my suitcase between shirts and sweaters. I told Victoria I had no idea of how to thank him, and she said I ought to write him a note, telling him I loved him. He thought, she told me, that people merely wanted him to help advance their career in letters and cared not a damn for him except as a power. I wrote him a note, on the overnight boat to Dublin, and said I loved him. When I returned to London in the spring, I had a letter from him in my hand, telling me to come and visit. I carried it in my pocket over my heart.

In a third-class compartment on the night train early in January 1957, I set off for Venice. For eight hot, stinking hours, in the company of a pregnant woman, her farting husband, two American soldiers, and the acrid odors of rotting orange peels, stale coffee, and sweat, I ground off to Venice. I looked out the window and saw my face reflected in the glass: pasty, tired, disenchanted.

The soldiers snored; the pregnant lady fell on my shoulder with the weight of a club rolled in garlic. The morning came boorishly out of the dark, and the two Americans and I stood in the corridor looking dumbly into the formless dawn.

We decided to share a room in Venice for the three days they'd be there on leave. Our room was in a hotel near the Ponte des Consorzi. A tall window overlooked a canal flowing darkly past the stone wall of a church. It was a cavernous room, with high ceilings and stuffed with gilt furniture. I smelled the sea. A sunbeam fell on the edge of the windowsill.

I left alone to search out the Piazza San Marco and its church. In front of the side entrance to the basilica is a sweet *piazzetta*, a fountain, rough stone pavement, and a marvelous door going into a church. I took that little *piazzetta* for the Piazza San Marco. I had expected a vast space surrounded by galleries, cafés, and the great domes of St. Mark's shimmering in alarums of sea light. I was quite content: if that was it, that was it. But out of the corner of my eye, inching in, like an orange shadow, I saw the sky and the corner of the facade of the basilica. I rushed into the piazza as if I were falling into a blazing canyon. In a wilderness of color, light, fish air, domes, mosaics, birds, and the great horses on the roof, the world like a dolphin rode on the surface of my soul.

I could not sleep. I lay awake, awaiting the dawn. The night had banished the glory, and I could not shut my eyes, but the memory of the light and gold and lagoon startled my nerves. I had never known such a thing before. Beauty, well, beauty was there, in that thing, in that tree, in the sky, in a painting, in a body, but I had never known beauty in me, living within my body, rushing at me with a furious, cunning, relentless desire. I walked all day, touching the walls and mosaics, looking at the water, smelling the air, staring at bodies, leaning out of myself like a tiger let loose from a cage.

Peggy Guggenheim gave me a dinner party in her palazzo on the Grand Canal (I had a letter of introduction from Dorothy Van Ghent). In her drawing room, I was pinned to the couch by an immense contessa whose neck and wrists were ringed with enormous emeralds and rubies. We dined on curry, and I thought myself quite grand in this brilliant world. Dorothy had said I would like Peggy, and indeed I did. Clothed in a sari, she sat at the head of the table beside the marquis de Cuevas.

At dessert, my garter snapped (my French grandmother insisted I wear garters) and slipped into my shoe. After supper we descended into the cellar to look at Peggy's collection of paintings, and as we got up from the table my garter slipped over my shoe and onto the floor. The contessa pointed at it. I unhooked it and kicked it into a corner beside the stair. One of Peggy's artists, a young Italian named Tancredi, who was present at the dinner, had some of his paintings hung among the Pollocks, Ernsts, Rothkos, and Gottliebs. I knew nothing about modern art. I had had a glimpse of Rothko during my years at Columbia, when I wandered into a gallery on Fifty-seventh Street and left thinking the walls were being repainted and the job had not yet been finished. Later in the day, when I was drawn back to the gallery by some sense that I had missed something, I realized I had been looking at Rothkos. When Tancredi asked me how I liked his paintings, I pointed at one and said, "It is like a forest on the edge of a sea." He said I was hopeless.

> O'Gorman: I see in that painting some nuns walking down a stair in a forest.
>
> Tancredi: There are no nuns or forests in that painting.
>
> O'Gorman: But I do see objects. I look for them in paintings and if I do not see objects I don't see anything.
>
> Tancredi: Objects. *Je deteste l'objet.*
>
> O'Gorman: I love objects.

I walked Tancredi back to his apartment after dinner, and as we crossed the Academia Bridge he bent down and picked up a bit of cloth on the steps.

> Tancredi: *C'est l'objet.*
>
> O'Gorman: Are you a Catholic?
>
> Tancredi: *Non, je suis un Platonist.* Are you a Catholic?
>
> O'Gorman: *Oui. Je suis un Catholic. Je suis un Aristotelian.*

I had found reason in Beauty. Poetry became the ark for the world rather than a carriage for my rampaging self. In the Academia, on the bridges across the canals, in the churches, standing in a piazza as the sun loosed a cornice from a shadow, gobbling down fettuccine and drinking wine, kneeling to get the host in San Marco as the wind tore through the portals carrying the smell of the lagoon and the sea over the blazing marble and mosaics — then I learned my first lessons about the world: it is no less dear than paradise, and any paradise must mirror it.

On the night of my journey to Rome, the American soldiers went out to dinner. One remained behind, wanting to share a dream he'd had. He had lost his virginity just the week before in Rome. The girl he had made love to was a whore. In his dream, just as he had entered her and reached orgasm, the curtains of the room parted, and there was his mother looking down on him and his whore. He had the dream every night; just as he was about to take off his pants, he said, there was his mother, watching, always watching.

He and I walked out and looked at the lagoon. A funereal barge piled with flowers slid past on water, still as slow-running liquid glass. Electric wire strung from poles sunk into the water crossed over the depths like threads held by a water god, all-powerful, sublimely calm. Nothing has ever been as quiet as those waters of the lagoon; they seemed to slope into the distance, like a rhino rising from his pool. I thought of Torcello too, for the contessa sitting next to me during Peggy Guggenheim's dinner had told me that the sea

around Torcello had risen up centuries ago and submerged a Roman temple to Venus. If you look, she
said, into the depths of the canal beside you as you step
off the boat onto the island, you will see a Doric capital
break through the surface. I, of course, believed her.

I came upon Rome in a flash and devoured it.

I had imagined Rome, but I had never taken the
trouble to look at a map. In my mind, the Vatican was
in the center of Rome, surrounded by a high wall. (I
dreamed the night before I went to Rome that I rode a
bicycle around it until I fell from exhaustion, trying to
find a way in.) I knew no history. Rome did not exist in
time or space. I had reserved a room in a convent on
the Viale Vaticano, beyond the Tiber and across from
the Vatican wall. I went out into the city, searching for
Rome as I would an Easter egg.

I stood by the Tiber and looked up toward St. Peter's, wishing I could breathe in the city all at once. I always consummate a thing before the event is off its
feet, anticipate the end of a journey before it begins. I
stood in a whirl of traffic and light and did not know
what to do. I walked back to the convent and took the
turning that led to the piazza of the Vatican. The stones
of the Bernini colonnade were wet, and a gray light
seeped through them, out into the square where the
fountains, the obelisk, and the facade of the basilica,
serene in the dark, were three points in space. Three
forms, three perfect marks of my imagination's holiest

dreams. (The Piranesi on the classroom walls in Bradford, there in front of me; the wilderness, the stones,
the water.) The fountains, leafy antennae bred of
stone, lanced the dark and shot small streams of silver
water down onto the pavement. The sun had begun to
set, and the Roman dark had come up out of the earth.
The obelisk was surrounded by a low iron fence; on my
left and right, the fountains (Rome is divine in rain), in
front of me the facade, and above, in the shifting,
cloudy sky of January, the dome.

Rome is eternal, temporal, pagan, lucid, classical,
murky, ageless, modern, mortal, filthy; in a word, it is,
as Stark Young said, a "ciborium." All modes, styles,
ideas, theology, philosophy, dwell there, each domi-
nant, each irresistible. I wrote of this confusion and order when I went to the opening of the Second Vatican
Council in 1962.

There will never be any way to explain Rome. Christ
and Nero, Pallas Athena and Saint Peter, meet there.
The spirits of all the gods have equal rights in Rome,
though one may love one God more than another. No
God is fool enough to take it all for his own. It is an
eternal city, and *eternal* is an adjective for all the gods to
share. Rome is a surfeit of everything: children, soldiers,
sailors, monks, women, cats, diplomats, cars, tourists,
students, popes, saints, demons, martyrs, princes, pre-
tenders, palaces, beggars, movie stars, beatniks, poets,
painters, and mothers. Rome has nothing to do with

time; each epoch still possesses the city, each mystery cult, each sacred sentiment and myth, weaves in and out of light and darkness. Michelangelo and Nervi, Silone and Tasso, the marionettes in the Borghese gardens and Verdi in the Caracalla, the snake in the Mithraeum and the chains of St. Peter, each is an emblem of the city. Rome leaps out of itself; the hills that shine beyond the harbor, vineyards and monks, with equal gaiety bring the eye up, beyond, out of the noise — and Rome is the noisiest city in Christendom: Vespas, and the *Romani* shouting, scratching, praying; the beautiful *Romani*, using space as if it were all in Rome and running out each day. Rome is eternal because, as we were taught to believe of eternity, nothing there ever seems to come to an end. Pasta is the food of Rome; it is eternal, for one can do with pasta what one wishes; put into it, over it, and through it all growing things. In the hands of a great Roman cook it becomes like Proteus, multiform and mythological.

I woke one morning with demons pricking at my nerves. Those raucous seeds of loneliness had started to grow again. At noon I took a bus to a Franciscan monastery in the hills of Umbria; it perched on the top of an arid hill, with a view of fields that stretched for miles over the valley. I was greeted with love and gentle hospitality by monks, who believed the Christ still comes to them in the guise of an unexpected guest. I took a chair from the whitewashed cell they gave me and propped it against the low cloister wall and sat there for hours in the sun, looking down into the valley. I ate hard bread and occasionally a piece of rancid chocolate. The light and air were a balm there on the precipice as I looked down into a countryside where farmers forced life from a land that seemed rough and tired. Just as night fell one day, I thought I saw a man, in a field below me far away, lift a shovel and strike another man on the head. I thought I saw him fall and the other flee. But I know I dreamed it, for while I was there I read Genesis and thought a good deal about Adam and Eve, Cain and Abel, and the rituals of the first day. The sun poured out the last flower of its heat, and mist and dark clouds rose up and breathed in the monastery. A crow settled on the bell tower (I could watch birds fly at the level of the cloister garden, so high it was; I saw what the birds up two thousand feet saw; that astonished me!)

In my cell with its pine desk, porcelain basin, and canvas cot, I grew back into life. The sun, the simple food, the birds, the views, were bread and wine to me. I returned to Rome, the angels and demons less red-eyed, and as I walked up the Janiculum, a surge of physical and spiritual pleasure in the world bowled me over, and I thought, had I dared, I could have floated out over the city, my heart and mind were so caught up in dreams of love and poetry and the Roman style.

This city, this city! I would have loved her had she never existed. I would have traveled to her gates had she never built walls to hold them. I would have praised the color of her elephantine green pines were I blind, and would have sung to every man I met the songs of her myths and river were I dumb and had Aeneas never lived. I would have named her Rome and counted her hills to seven had she never been founded, and had I no alphabet or numbers. She is the inevitable city; the present habitation of mystery; the thoroughfare and palisade, the savannah and plateau, the metropolis and campsite of what I trust must be the best image I will know on earth of heaven.

I love the silence, though Rome is a labyrinth of sound. The motorcycle in all its dreadful monotony prowls the city like a drunken monster bee, but it is soon vanished into the light like thunder into the galaxies. Silence in Rome is not the absence of sound but the presence of silence, tangible as the fabric of the facades of the Piazza di Spagna that, at dusk, on the day of a brilliant sun setting, holds the sounds of mortar and stone, lintel and cornice, portal and rooftop, the instant before they fall toward the foraging dark.

I love the impenetrable forms of her interior life and the secrets of the streets that turn on themselves and open like shelves of dark colored glass on fountains and plains of crested shadows. Nothing in Rome grows worn with remembrance. When I return to a market, to a flight of steps, to a courtyard, to a hillside, to a junction of a temple and its enfolding sacral light, a new order of feeling visits me, though I might have been to that very place just hours before. There is always a plateau I have never reached, a labyrinth of febrile, sensuous delight I have never entered.

Friends tell me how noisy and dirty Rome has become, how changed she is from the old days before
World War II, when the pastoral style still hovered over
the countryside beyond the walls, but I say damn *that*
Rome. I did not know that city. I know *this* Rome, the
Rome hemmed in by the modern world, an arrogant,
brazen, sweet, divine village of villages, where the glory
of man and God's glory reign as if everything were its
own perfect hierarchy, and no creed and no philosophy
dare assert dominion. All creeds would claim Rome;
none deserve her, none can ever own her.

She has been hacked up and vulgarized, raped
and mocked by vandals, shopkeepers, popes, pilgrims,
and tourists with hands and spirits of guttersnipes. Her
air is polluted by the spittle of exhaust fumes, and her
river writhes with mud, but she knocks them off, those
whores, those gnats, those bunions, as a great lady or a
general or mighty stallion knocks off pests of the common light.

Rome is immortal, and all that attends her is;
Rome is mortal, and all that attends her is: the gods, the
Holy Stair, the pillars, the stone, the burial places in
moss and anemones, the ceremony, its altars, everything is hawker of the world and paradise. Rome holds
sway over me because she is my guide to the beautiful
and holy; my flesh and spirit find bivouac there. I am
held like a toad in her ruined frame, in the forehead of
her maimed and stunning artifice and life. Rome is the
shape of a passionate distraction. Everywhere I look
there are deliriums of perception.

Rome leaps in and out of time. Light, water, stone,

air, and flowers cloister the nerves and burn through to the soul, proclaiming the triumph of beauty and man over the demon and death. The cloister envelops the imagination. The vortex leaps into silence. The mind is pushed against the tides of feeling, is swept away by a fancy of, say, Borromini or Bramante, who took stone and bent it into a grain of air, angelic and aquatic, that sweeps over and into the flesh and mind.

Rome, the prismatic barque.

I first unlocked the inside wooden shutters, then pulled open the window, unlocked the outer shutters, and leaned out and looked up the Via Sistina to the obelisk at the top of the Spanish Steps. Before I slept, I had closed the two sets of shutters tight, so that the morning light would stun me with a grand shattering of the prism of night. It was going to be a bright day. The sky, its dark blue held under the thin silver-orange shadows of the dawn, gleamed above and touched the tops of the lovely ocher buildings across the way. It was six, and the power of Roman light inched across my body and broke within, urging me out. The day had been sliced through with an ivory knife and laid open before me, an orange on a lapis lazuli platter.

I drew the shutters closed and lay upon my bed, rose up after a moment, and opened them again, unfolding the mystery a second time as I might have gazed, after love, upon the body of a creature I knew was infinite in allure and could be tasted forever as if for the first time.

In the morning I climbed to the roof of St. Peter's,

then to the dome, walked about the nave, and at noon to the Piazza Navona, that beached marble-and-clay frigate built on the foundation of Domitian's Circus Agonalis. The sun swung from church steeple to balcony, from balcony to rows of geraniums, from geraniums to the pavement, as if the Navona held the sun and offered it to all creation, waiting upon the earth like a chalice to receive it.

Rome speaks against my Puritan spirit. Olive oil, fresh grated cheese, garlic, ripe pears, Roman bodies fitted tight into the clothes they will bear with them to heaven, the gutters running with waste, my breakfast roll, marmalade, bitter coffee, orange juice, murky and tart, seeds floating on top, tasting of the earth. In Rome, no distinction between my dream of the world and what the world is.

At eight in the evening I sat on a stone outside a gate to the garden of the Palazzo Borghese in the Largo della Fontanella di Borghese. A cat had climbed atop the head of a Roman soldier, who lay on his back, his face shattered, the marble of his chest and legs covered over with ivy. A fountain, stagnant and glistening, had gathered the light of evening onto its oily surface. Statues, bits of ancient carved stone, lay awash in the grass, clamant runes, and vines and flowers hung on the massive walls, spores of time, delicate, yet rooted into the mortar like filaments of carved, painted gold.

The scent of wet stone, cats, roses, grass, and the covering of lichen and moss struck me with a great fit of mortal pleasure; I laid my face against the grill and felt the moist night on my lips.

*   *   *

The cry of scallions, garlic, carrots, melons, peppers, and green beans rose up into the sun like oils on seaweed, like dew on caterpillars. The smell, the density, the dry leaf of garlic, the ribbed bark of carrots, the green whip of stem in the cluster of scallions, the heavy breath of the melons, split, lying on their sides, their pulplike intestines and seeds packed into the center, fireballs of peppers and onions hanging from the roofs of the stalls, where fish smells and raw meat crackled against the mute agape harvest.

I walked to the remnants of the Porta di Ripetta, that shard of a grand water stair that used to sweep down to the Tiber to a quay that received produce from Umbria and Sabina. From the glassed-in loggia of a crumbling palace, two busts, one of a lady, one of a gentleman, in togas, stared out over the river. A man stripped to his undershorts stretched out in languid peace on a pavement that ran along the brown churning waters of the river; the shadows of the leaves above him played over his body like knives cutting shadows into his muscle. An old fisherman left his pole and peed into the bark of a dying tree woven into the walls of the embankment, and a girl embraced her lover and ran her fingers down his chest and rested them on his crotch.

I returned to the Albergo by way of the Trevi Fountain. The sun had cast its light into the waters like a hot poker and raised them up with lapidary grace into the fiddling dusk. I watched the explosion as the little sea of the Trevi and its petrified horses galloped into

the dark. Everything here. Rome, the manifest Al-
leluia.

On the last day of this journey to Rome, I pushed myself to the Campo dei Fiori, where I found the flower
market in lusty progress. I was starved, and the sun of
noon had laid its heel in me. Passing through the
beaded curtain entrance of the Carbonara, I climbed to
the second floor and sat at a table overlooking the
square. Sun spilled through the shutters that had been
closed upon the noon light. I rested my elbows on the
tablecloth, still moist from the night's washing. A dish
of pasta often rescued me from despair. I ordered one I
loved: folded squares of dough filled with spinach, garlic, cheese, and herbs, the edges browned in the oven,
piping hot, drenched in a sauce of heavy cream and
served in a white bowl on a serving plate painted with
flowers and bees. I brooded with enfolding joy and
gazed upon the salad of ripe sliced tomatoes and moz-
zarella cheese splashed with olive oil, deep yellow with
a tinge of green, as if it were a holy, vatic offering. I
knocked down two carafes of wine, coffee, and a dish
of fruit. At three, I pushed open the window shutters
and the fountains flashed in the air, filled with smells of
fish, ripe fruit, roses, cheese, and a trace of urine. The
heat wrapped about me; the wine had felled me with a
lovely, garlic drowsiness. I poured out the last drops of
wine and tottered down the stairs into the empty
square. Boys played at soccer, and some leaped naked
into the fountains. I walked to St. Peter's and watched

the dome, like a fluted disc of dark — oiled, olive, silver — lean, and vanish into the sky. In bed, I opened
the shutters wide and let night cover me. I slept till six,
when the alarm went off and the sun touched me simply, like a belled anemone, on the brow.

10

Mount Saviour

W HEN I RETURNED FROM EUROPE IN NOVEMBER 1957, I had decided to become a priest. I ought to have known something was wrong with my decision if I had to go to such lengths to hide it. But I thought the angels must be dotty with pleasure to think that a poet was ready to give up every randy appetite for a life of work, prayer, and searing detachment from, I thought then, the world. In the priestly life, I intended to be loved and to love the one to whom I had a fixed and lucid bond: Christ, who was the world, poetry, and the imagination.

I lived a secret life. I scattered false clues to hide my tracks: I went about with four different girls and pretended I'd marry one of them; I studied Latin in Princeton, but only, I told everyone, to qualify for graduate school; I hid books on prayer and theology and had mail from abbots, bishops, and seminaries sent to a friend's apartment.

I visited first in my pilgrimage St. Joseph's Seminary in Dunwoodie, New York. I snuck out of the city and made my way in a heavy rain by train, cab, and foot to that enchanted demi-world of my childhood. I had passed by it when I was very young and saw it from the back seat, where I sat wedged in between my sisters and Lydia on our trips to New York. It stood on a hill like some Arthurian castle, surrounded by lawns, volleyball courts, and pairs of young men walking, hands behind their backs, heads bowed, among the shadows. When we drove by, I turned my face away; it lurked in me always. A landmark; a totem; an enchanted paysage.

I knocked on the door; a seminarian opened it and led me to a dark, black, wood-paneled drawing room to await the rector, who would decide on my worthiness. He came like a tumbrel through the door and sat on the edge of a long oak table, his hands upon it, palms down, his face turned toward me, looking over my head at a crucifix on the wall.

"What do you think the priesthood is?" he asked.

I don't remember what I answered, but I think it might have been rather too rich an answer; a mixture of love, piety, poetry, and a vague, hostile passion for sanctity. He got up, hands still on the table, bent over it, looked into my eyes, walked to the window, pushed aside a heavy velvet curtain, and told me a story.

"Some years ago, when you were still a boy, my nephew Tony went mountain climbing in Switzerland. He was a *poet*." (My first mistake was in telling the rector I was a poet.) He asked me, before he went on with his story, what I would do on a Saturday night when it was time to hear confessions. Would I go and sit on the docks and look up into the moon and forget my pastoral duties if a poem "came on me"? I told him I did not work at poetry like that; my fits of inspiration did not take me off to the docks in the moonlight.

"Well," he continued, talking as he looked out the window, "one day my nephew went out in the morning and did not return." There was silence. The rector looked at me. I looked at him. "The poet did not return."

I said, "What happened, Father, did he get lost?"

"No, he did not get lost." I waited for him to go on. He had come away from the window and sat down again. "Days later they found his body at the foot of a cliff. It seemed he had fallen off a cliff." The rector gave great weight to "seemed." He looked at me and said again, "It *seemed* he had fallen."

He stared, and I tried to understand what he was trying to get across, then suddenly it came to me: My God, he's telling me his "poetic" nephew, bitten by the muse, had jumped and killed himself. He was telling me that if there were a place I ought not to be, that place was a seminary, for poets tend to sit on docks, neglect their duties, and, if a quirk in the blood happens to urge them, jump off things. Foiled, I left the seminary like a leper cast outside the precincts of the temple.

I wandered from diocese to diocese, from bishop to bishop. No one would have me. I think I always seemed too poetic, too ambivalent in my attitudes toward the rigors of seminary life, though I was quite happy and ready to accept whatever limitations on my freedom the life of a priest might impose. I simply couldn't get my docility across to anyone. When the possibility of a commonplace priesthood seemed unlikely, the Monastery of Mount Saviour in Elmira, New York, a community of contemplative Benedictine monks who farmed and prayed in an Arcadian landscape — so I heard — tempted me with promises of the Lord, the Church, and Ritual. I visited them, bearing my secret hidden tightly amid my poems, dreams, and imaginings of holiness.

The monastery buildings, high on a hill surrounded by fields green in the prime of late summer crops, ranged simple and clear as stones in rain, with views of rivers, mountains, and valleys falling away gently in the distance. The land was rapt with the smell of wheat and honeysuckle and silence. The bells, the lowing of cattle, the sun, the bright green, brown world, like scenes on Limoges plates, sang at my fingertips. I said to myself, "This is the place. I will come here and live the rest of my life." But I had no idea what I meant except that my heart yearned so for a consummation; sexual, poetic, intellectual. I wandered over the land for the week I visited the monastery, watching the light on the chapel walls, following the cattle as they rummaged over the hills. I sat in the hay in the barn, the smell of molasses and forage luring me into dreams of song and ecstasy. And prayer. I assaulted the abbot with letters, telegrams, and sudden trips to the monastery, until he said I might come there as a novice, if I submitted myself first to a psychiatrist to

discover if there might not be quirks in my spirit that
would disturb the cloister.

In February 1959 I sailed again to Europe on a "farewell
tour." I went first to Dublin, where I had arranged to
take a Rorschach inkblot test from a Dr. Earle, who had
given it to Yeats. (When I failed to yield up to him the
conventional responses to the blots, he told me that not
since Yeats had he heard such fantastic perceptions: No
one else but you and Yeats saw, he said, pointing to a particular blot, such a figure. We did not see the same figure, he told me, but we saw a figure no one else had ever
seen.) The abbot at Mount Saviour said he'd accept as a
judgment on my fitness an acceptable result from my
session with Earle. Though the friend in Dublin who
sent me to Earle was, I know now for certain, homosexual, he and I were skilled enough in deception to hide it
even from Earle. My friend had taken the test as well.
    Earle's office was a little hut in a secluded part of
his garden. The trek from the front door of his house to
that hut was long and complicated. I felt that I was going to be grilled, and heaven knows what he would
find. I was confident that I had all the "forbidden" stuff
packed away and could bluff it well enough to prevent
any leak. I had to go through his sitting room, across a
lawn, and through a door in a brick wall to find him sitting behind a low wooden table, his clubfoot propped
up on a bench and the blots in a pile before him. (I did
not know it then, but he was dying of cancer.) He
greeted me. I sat down. He lifted up a card. He told me

to say what first came to me. I must not worry about logic, nor must I waste time "figuring it out." The cards simply set the mind adrift, he said, they do not judge. He took the blots lightheartedly.

At first I saw nearly all the right things. I missed a penis, a vagina, demons, and a witch, but on the whole I was doing well. "You and Yeats do badly on the blots in the long run, since your minds never work outside their creative imagination and meditations."

When I read the results, I discovered that I saw too much serenity and too little evil. I ought to have seen more devils and fewer calm seas. When the colors turned from black to color, I took no note of the change: a bad sign, indicating some deprivation of a sense of evil. (O'Gorman has an underdeveloped sense of evil, he told my gay Irish friend.) I saw liturgical symbols, scenes from Bosch's *Garden of Earthly Delights* (I had been in Madrid in 1957 and saw that painting at the Prado). I ought to have seen imps. I saw flying fish when I ought to have seen an erect penis. I did see an erect penis, but was embarrassed to say so. I left him unsettled, for I did not like to think I had an underdeveloped sense of evil. I felt like an erotic misfit, a poseur, a poet with a blighted imagination.

When the abbot saw the report from Earle, he wrote me that I might come to Mount Saviour when I returned. I have often wondered if my friend who sent me to Earle doctored the results. I knew that somewhere in that hour or so with him, Earle got to the root of my being. But since my friend was a priest, he took pity on an aspiring priest. And he knew, of course, that

I'd not do sexual mischief; the girls and boys of the countryside would be safe; monasteries always fear the invasion of the occasional queer. Before I made my move on Mount Saviour, some fellow was rumored to have been found in a compromising idyll, and another had tried to burn down a barn.

I returned to America and found, in Margaret Marshall's office at Harcourt Brace, my first volume of poetry: *The Night of the Hammer.* It came out, was hardly reviewed, but as I got ready to "become a Benedictine monk," I got this letter from my cousin Leonie Knoedler:

Dear Ned

Thank you very much for the copy of your poems. Poor critic as I am, I feel you have the authentic gift and all the makings in mind and feeling. What a wonderfully difficult and rare art it is!

Again thank you for sending the poems and thank you for being a poet. I am sure that our common ancestor, Judge Richard O'Gorman, if he could look down, with his deep love of Shakespeare, would be happy, and would love the splendidly expressive line: *"when it seems Lear did mightily by the hurricane."* The seed blows in mysterious ways!

The day my mother sailed to France for a holiday in the fall of 1958, I left this world for another: the Mount Saviour monastery. A world where God would govern me, my body, and my poor erotic soul.

*   *   *

I had visited Mount Saviour a number of times over the years, to pray, to meditate, to join the monks in their liturgical life. I spent the first week as a pre-novice at Mount Saviour in a guest house. The monks had no idea what to do with me. They had grown fond of me and decided to humor my monastic fancy. No one thought I'd "make it" to a cowl. They thought I was a playboy, a poet, rich, disreputable, and made for no life but a saloon and a ball. I took my new life with seriousness, and did not know they thought me such a fool.

In the fields, I was the happiest I had ever been in my life. I was alone there, and the air and light rumbled about me as I worked in the wild eye of the hills. I spent the first month digging ditches — irrigation ditches, ditches for water pipes — and I rigged up a system of ropes and pails to get dirt out of the ditches that were too deep and narrow to throw it out with a shovel.

In the chapel, I was the demon's easy prey. In the fields the nerves and mind flowered. I shoveled manure, pitched hay, cleaned latrines, and had no trouble with my dreams and my spirit as long as my body was intent on work. In the chapel, I went into sulks. I wanted to write poems. The novice master said no: it would be a distraction. I tucked the muse away, but he'd not be still. I worried the prior. It is not my nature to be quiet and self-possessed. The master of novices popped tranquilizers in my mouth that I'd keep under my tongue and spit out when he left. I could not sleep and dreaded the sound of the bells that called me to pray.

In the fields, I discovered I was very strong. I loved the notion of my body pulling against the earth. My muscles grew. I looked at myself in the bathroom mirrors — no mirrors allowed in the cells — and watched my arms grow hard and my belly firm. I thrust a heavy iron bar into the ground and forced enormous rocks out of the loam. I lifted a sledgehammer high above my head and held it there as long as I could, then let it fall, cracking the rock at the center, bits of it shooting into the air, stinging my face.

Deer, rabbits, sleeping rattlesnakes under rocks, birds, bees, were the runes that bore me through the day. I learned the delights of work, the life of the land, and the demands of the agricultural Lord. I wished to be a monk immediately. I was not allowed to wear even the simple habit of the novice, and the moment I would feel the black cloth fall about my shoulders seemed a galaxy away. Had I been less ravenous, I'd perhaps be a monk now.

My closest friend during the happy days of my "enclosed life" was Brother Stephen. I saw him sitting alone at breakfast one morning as I went out to chase a cow that had broken out of her pen. The sunlight fell on the rough wood, the polished cutlery, the bright fieldstone floor, all clear as grass caught in ice, and Stephen in the midst of it, looking at his food, deep in love with the Lord.

I could not ever flee the memory of Peter. He followed me about, in and out of chapel, in the fields, into my room, beside me on my cot, and it became quite intolerable to banish him and be a monk, simply; he was within me, too, as much as the Lord, and one day when I was near tears I went to talk to Brother Stephen. I knew he would understand, for he was queer, too. I sensed it — the way he stood, walked, looked about him. I told him of my love and how it had still the power of besotting me. He said: You must remember this story. There was once a wise Chinese monk who said to a man who came to complain about a bird that followed him about, circling over his head until he thought he would go mad: "Let the bird be, he will soon tire of you, but do not let him build a nest in your hair."

I provoked my novice master, Father Anthony, by ignoring all manner of monastic etiquette. I ran naked to the showers, I read Proust late into the night, cowering under my sheets and blankets to conceal the light of a torch I had filched from the barn. I never made my bed; my cell stank of manure, and my little desk was a squalid heap of flowers, books, a rattlesnake's skin, a rabbit foot, autumn leaves, and a bowl of holy water.

Finally enough was enough. My novice master thought I would have a nervous breakdown, so ravenous was I to be a monk. The prior, one night after I had finished my chores in the barn, told me that I must leave the monastery, and on a cold morning in November of 1958 at first light I was driven to the local airport and put on a plane back home.

But I had visited for a slash of time my idea of the ideal earthly kingdom. Still in my reveries of these odd moments of bliss I have known in my life, I remember the rocks I split there, the cows I milked, the sound of

Gregorian chant as the monks and I prayed the monastic hours, and the shadow of Peter rushing past me in the fields. I was dwelling in a sacred place, and learned there the ways of carnal and divine desire and of the impossibility of it all.

I learned to loathe academic life. I had taught at Manhattan College in 1959 and Brooklyn College. I was offered tenure at both, but the thought of correcting essays and teaching John Donne horrified me. I helped edit a radical (for those days) Catholic magazine and spent three months in South America, sent there as a cultural ambassador by my cousin Harry McPherson, and the senators Eugene McCarthy and William Fulbright. Once there, I made a great mess of everything by spending my per diem giving lunch to Communists and learning that American foreign policy in Chile, Brazil, and Argentina was oppressive, tied to right-wing ideology, and generally corrupt. I wrote about it in the *National Catholic Reporter* and lost my cousin's friendship. He was a close friend of Lyndon Johnson's and thought that I had betrayed his trust. I had.

Nothing loomed more clearly than that I was destined to do nothing very much with my life. I slept anywhere I was given a bed, and once discovered that I had but one pair of shoes, and the soles were so tattered that I was walking barefoot on the pavement. But I was saved from a derelict's life by the great Broadway producer Roger Stevens, who let me live in his flat in the Carlyle Hotel. He was in Washington, D.C., during those months as the director of the Kennedy Center.

But being a hobo was my future until that corrective day when I met Father Jim Sugrue. What follows is a history of my life with children and neighbors on 129th Street from Park Avenue to Lenox Avenue.

Part Two

Sometimes I pray to you God about special things in my life that I tell no one else. To my surprise they usually come true too. Like the other day I prayed for something very special to me and it seems to be coming true. At first I really didn't get the sense of what God wanted me to do, but then later I prayed a lot at church. Two Sundays ago I came about fifteen minutes before my religion class started and sat in church praying. Don't ask me what I prayed about because you know I will not tell you. I will not tell anyone. I just want you to know I pray about things that are very special to me in my life right now.

— Ricky O'Gorman, age 10

A certain number of years lived in misery are sufficient to construct a sensibility.

— Albert Camus

11

Ricky

WHEN I WAS THIRTEEN YEARS OLD, I was playing croquet on the lawn of my family's farm in Vermont. Aunt Claude set down her wineglass on the grass and whacked my ball into the weeds. She picked up her glass and tottered into the house to fill it to the brim from the ever-replenished carafe on the sideboard in the dining room.

I stood alone, mallet in my hand, and said loud, *"Je serai seul toute ma vie."* It rose up out of my soul, unbidden by any present sorrow — my childhood was always sunk in lamentation — and I had not remembered it until one day after a lover had left me, decades after the croquet game. I looked at his picture on my desk, touched the emptiness about — his possessions gone, his clothes, his razor, his books — and said aloud again: *"Je serai seul toute ma vie,"* and to this day it explains everything to me. It does not bring despair or grief, for I am a happy fellow. It does bring a balm, the comfort of truth.

1966. The second part of my life began and revolved for forty years around my storefront school, the Ricardo O'Gorman Garden and School.

When I write about Harlem now, in these reveries of the past, I write about my son, Ricky, my kidnapped child. His life and his death are the history of my spirit, in its mammoth effort to bring one child out of the dark and into the light. It was a history of moments of joy, as he grew and flourished, and a history too of forces beyond him, within him, that spoiled the journey and cast him into the abyss. These reflections about Ricky, his family, my building up of his home with me, break even now my heart with remorse and a sense of failure, as well as a sense of the absurd. For what I tried to do was linked to my class, to my sensibilities, to my certainty that if I had escaped the abyss as a child, I could help my "kidnapped son" escape. It was a flamboyant adventure to put a hex on the life of loneliness and isolation that I had predicted as my fate.

I picked him up every morning from his grandmother's apartment. He was just two years old. I carried him to the storefront school I had founded on Madison Avenue and cared for him until about three in the afternoon, when I returned him home. One morning I was preparing to take the children on a trip to the country and saw Rick sitting on the doorsill with a neighbor, who had decided he could not accompany us since he was not toilet trained. He wept, and I took him along anyway. As days went by, I watched him decline into an infant torpor; I decided I would give him a proper home.

The children of the oppressed have no surrogate will to snatch them from deterioration. Families often disintegrate with such ferocity that the children get caught in the debris, their sensibilities smother, and the will to thrive dissolves into quick despair. Yes, little children experience despair; it burrows into them, like worms eating away at their joy. Ricky was on the verge. I often wonder, with rue and anguish, whether I got him too late, whether decay and death had already established their dominion in his fragile being. But take him home I did. Asked no one permission, just picked him up and decided to save him.

It was a sort of kidnapping. I think that was clear to him as he grew up, that he was a kidnapped child, snatched from the natural family that had no way to see to his care and little hope. Had he lived with them, he would end up lost, flayed with failure and sorrow.

Ricky lived with his grandmother, his two brothers, and a sister in "the projects" on 135th Street. His mother was about, flashing through the apartment, but never there more than it took to open and close a door, a bird of passage. His father went away the day Rick was born, some said to Jamaica, and never saw Rick. Rumors now and then that he was about never produced him. Rick was curious about him and asked me when he was five if I would take him to Jamaica to search for him. I did, and we wandered about, "looking." Ricky led me to where he thought he might be. He stopped now and then to ask if anyone knew a Mr. Frazier. He kept on asking, and then one day I knew he had given up that pilgrimage. He never asked about him again.

But I was not alone in guarding Ricky. There was my companion, who was as determined as I to bring him into our life. The first weekend Ricky came to stay, we bathed him, and the tub was ringed with dirt. From then on it was quite simple: Ricky moved in with us.

All of a sudden, Rick began to touch, seek, embrace the world. (And *that* is the moment a teacher builds upon.) We watched as he discovered that elastic bands snapped and stung, that Scotch tape stuck to his arm, that if he pulled an electric light cord, the lightbulb would flash on, and that when he flushed the john, *his* hand made it flush. I tricked him, or so I thought, by laying my hand upon his when he could not move the lever down. When the john flushed, he looked at me and said, "You did it. Me didn't." He set claim to his pillow at naptime, his blocks, his crayons, his paper, and pointed (as if he were a stargazer watching a new planet come into orbit) to his eyes, penis, knees, ears, and feet. "My feets, my peepee, my blocks!" He learned to clown and make me laugh. He figured out that mock tears and mock misery did get hugs and kisses from us. He pretended he was asleep when he wanted to get our eyes off him. There was not a rotten apple in his spirit anywhere.

Ricky's mother was a brilliant woman, and had she been favored with an education, with an acceptable beauty of place, and with kin who were not delivered up to hopelessness, she could have been an extraordinary creature. I knew just how smart she was, how adventurous in things of the mind, when she showed me her "Knowledge Book," a spiral notebook crammed with bits of "knowledge" that she picked up in her calm moments in the local public library. She would fetch a volume from the *Encyclopaedia Britannica*, open it at random, and copy down whole paragraphs from whatever topic she happened upon. It was written in a small, almost hieroglyphic hand, clear, exact, filling page after page. When she showed it to me, she was in travail, her being wracked with pain, her mind a bit askew, but in that book was her soul. She died when she was very young.

When he was a teenager, Rick had fled from his boarding school, and from me, and at his mother's urging returned to take care of her as she awaited death. Ricky and I buried her. Her casket, in a ramshackle church in the Bronx, was covered with a plastic sheet to keep the flies away from her face. He sat there and did not cry. I saw Ricky cry only twice, once when he heard my father had died, and again at my mother's funeral.

It was not easy taking care of Ricky. It all depended on how well we managed, X and I, the masquerade. We had so much to protect: Rick and his life, X's life with me, our reputation, me a schoolmaster and guardian of one little boy and what was going to be a constant interrogation by everyone about my life. So the smokescreens, the mirrors. My life was filled with joy, and Rick grew with grace into an enchanting creature. During the years in our little apartment, we did concoct a family, no matter what people did indeed think. ("Ned," one lady asked, "where do you sleep?") To offset that sort of reflection, we hung around some girls we knew, went on journeys with them and Rick to shift our friends' attention, if not their speculation, and often certain knowledge of my sexual relationship with X. And because X and I could not publicly affirm our love for each other, a desperate frustration overpowered us, and in the end X left, married, and Rick and I carried on.

When Ricky came to me out of the brutality of his life, I cared for him as I had never been cared for. The household I created for him contained all the rituals and order and beauty that had kept the poisons of my parents' manner from breaking me. I thought that, were I to give him all, he would be tamed by such a landscape. He had his glory years. He loved music and travel, and there was never a harsh word between us.

As he grew, though, I could see the hardness settle in. He simply stopped in his tracks, and then catastrophes began. The catastrophes, sexual and emotional, especially the terrible kinship with his mother, left him nowhere to go but to the underworld he entered with abandon.

After that it was all downhill, despite my efforts to comfort, to halt the slide. Then one day, when he was twenty-six, I held him in my arms on a gurney in the emergency room at St. Vincent's Hospital: seventy pounds, vomiting up swells of blood and tissue. He died, and I closed his eyes. But I will never be certain that the troubles that took him to his death might not have done their damage to his life had I left him where I found him and let him grow in his inherited wasteland. I screamed and screamed, and stood by as he was wrapped in plastic and hauled off to the morgue.

As his body floated out of the room, I remembered how he had run like a flare of spring light around the track of his boarding school. Might he have turned away from the damned adventures into the darkness that killed him had X and I and Rick been allowed to live together in domestic tranquillity, unscrutinized by rumors and the possibility of scandal? Perhaps in God's compassion there will be a time when the great articulation of homosexual love will seem as sweetly commonplace as the air we breathe.

12

Harlem: The Beginning

CHILDHOOD IS A GIFT THE GODS GIVE CHILDREN. It is as precious as the rubies they give the earth and the sun they give the spheres. It is each child's absolutely; as rare as a unicorn or a phoenix. One childhood to every child. Childhood is the form that upholds each child's life forever. If a man or a society taints a child's childhood, brutalizes it, strikes it down, and corrupts it with fear and bad dreams, he maims that child forever, and the judgment on that man and that society will be terrible and eternal.

I found this place called Harlem, looked around, and right away was struck by Harlem's children, their dreams, their beauty, and their suffering. Before I knew it, I was there at work. These children had not been given the gifts I had been given: clean sheets, good food, an inner life, and the vision children have of an unbounded, rich, joyous, mysterious world.

On July 8, 1966, I came to Harlem to work as a volunteer in a summer program sponsored by OEO, the Office of Economic Opportunity. I was given a class of thirty children, seven and eight years old, fresh from the public schools, with their cruelties, their bureaucracy, their noise, their boredom, and their racist paranoias. They came from the streets. The suffering, mystery, and beauty of a black child can best be understood, I think, by watching his life in the streets.

The schools fear the streets and the streets' laws and tests of life. Boards of education see schools in the cities of the dispossessed as places of detention, stern moral foundations to counteract the streets. The schools become *contra naturam*.

My first day was a hallucination. I had no idea what to say to a seven-year-old black child. Until then I had never walked down a Harlem street. It was terra incognita, and the people there were as strange to me as if I had landed one day, suddenly, out of a dream, in a village on another planet. The room I was to work in was a sea of children, seething with anger, distrust, and contempt. For them, I was simply another teacher, another ruler who'd set them down, line them up, and bellow something at them, ordering them to "learn." The reality, however, was that I was merely a fool poet, with nothing but poetry in his bag, hoping the energy and joy that brought poems from chaos would carry me to the children.

I offered them simple gifts: maps, flowers, records of foreign languages, films and slides of strange lands and animals. We sang together and walked the streets of the city every day, wandering wherever we wished, freely, in a tight little mob, tottering on the edges of sidewalks, peering into store windows, and feeling the skeleton of our friendship grow and take on sinew and delight.

(Teaching is an act — first of all — of friendship.)

I had lived in East Africa for three months in 1962, and told my children it was a grand place, filled with life and mystery and a people whose journey into freedom was an example to the world of courage and stupendous human vision. But no, my children thought Africa was a terrible place. Lon told me, "Them Africans is savages; them ate peoples and shooted tigers. They is black and ugly."

I said Africans were beautiful. A black friend told my class that he was an African from Kenya. Sherril looked at him and ran from the room.

"How many of you are happy that you're black?" No one raised his hand. "Do any of you want to be white?" They all raised their hands.

But my job was to teach, not to talk about Africa. Soon we could read maps. The children knew where Africa was, and they could point out the countries there, and the mountains. There were other maps. They could find Manhattan, too, and Queens, Staten Island, Moscow, Cairo, China, Vietnam, and the North and South Poles. One day I brought eighteen envelopes of herbs to class: sweet basil, arrowroot, dill weed, tarragon, paprika, thyme, chervil, marjoram, garlic, curry, laurel, rosemary, mace, cloves, nutmeg, black Java pepper, oregano, and salt. The children put out their hands, and I placed a little pinch of herb in each of them. Vincent, Vernon, Sara, Chuckie, Man, Arthur,

Xavier, Lisa, Nathaniel, Tricia, Melony, Babu, Kevin, Billy Boy, Kenya, Ami, Tina, Thomas, Dede, Sister, Damon, Julius, the Keller twins, screamed, laughed, sneezed, shivered with disgust and delight, and ran about throwing the herbs into the air, trampling them underfoot until the room was a garden of children gone wild with the smells of the earth.

The public schools and the decrees of the Board of Education know one rule: order, order, order. Joy, wonder, freedom, abandonment to the world, are perceived, even condemned, as revolutionary ideas. Children desire freedom far more than they desire alphabets and times tables. I firmly believe that alphabets and times tables are skills one builds *on* childhood — one does not build childhood on them. Children must first learn to love themselves and the world, and then, in their proper time, the various skills and crafts will take their place.

The public schools breed terrible things that destroy children: despair, violence (intellectual and physical), fear, and those multitudes of tricks and rituals that crush a child's sense of freedom and joy.

When I was a child, all the forces for good in me flourished; the darkness, the forces of destruction, violence, and despair breathed little clement air. The demons could not flourish long, or not long enough to take hold. In Harlem, the powers in a child that tend to destruction find clement atmospheres and flourish.

A school such as mine, in the cities of the dispossessed, hopes to free children, not imprison them. I want it to be a place of freedom and delight. Forged in a black community, from a black child's inner life, from the streets, such a place welcomes the tremendous energy and sensibility that are the black people's in the midst of every kind of disaster. The two schools I have "built" in Harlem in the past decades are places of freedom and delight.

The children assaulted my spirit. It was a sweet assault: hardy as herbs, fragile as spring blossoms, luminous as the wings of baroque angels. I tried exposing them to everything. (We even went to Tiffany's, and they shouted with delight when they spied a ruby and sapphire grasshopper. "Oh, Ned," said Melony, "there's the green monster we seed in the country." A saleslady took it out of the case, and we all touched it.)

They were ready for freedom and adventure. Knowledge was in them, ready to spring into life, would the land, the teachers, the boards of education, the police, the churches, and the political lunatics quit their assaults on their inner lives.

Anything I tried giving my class I would have to give through the mediation of the city. The city and Harlem were our teachers and our classroom.

I learned that summer that education was a process of liberating the self within the child; of freeing the genius there; of presenting to each child the enormous presence in him of a hero.

In the summer of 1966, on Madison Avenue and 129th Street, I came upon an empty storefront, used now and then by some neighborhood kids to while away the day. I was told I might use it as I saw fit when I returned to New York in the fall.

The ceiling was gutted with leaking pipes. The windows were covered with greasy iron gates, and the floor was rutted and slimy with dead roaches and jagged planks of wood.

I turned around on 127th Street and looked up Madison Avenue. One of the children, a violent, dark-willed, deranged, brilliant boy, stood beside a lamp-post. I waved at him. He stared. I waved again and turned toward him to say good-bye. When he saw me, he walked away. He walked up the avenue to 130th Street, waited for the light, crossed the street, and stood again beneath a lamppost, looking at me. I had stopped. He had no reason to wait for the light. The street was empty. He was asking me to follow and say something to him, but was afraid and didn't know yet that I was a friend. I waved. He smiled and ran.

On October 9, I walked back into the storefront. Inside, a dozen or so black kids lolled around in a haze of smoke and a clamor of transistors. They looked neither up nor down when I burst through the door, a lost man in their city, who knew nothing about poverty, suffering, and the ways of this vicious white world in a black man's life. I could not ask their help, and had I dared, they would have turned on me and told me to go to hell. I had to go through the ceremonies of their history, ceremonies my hieratic white life had spared me. That isolation nearly killed me.

"Hello, I'm Ned O'Gorman," I said. No one said a

word. I sat down at a long metal table and started to doodle. I had no idea what to do.

The dirty window annoyed me. Someone ought to wash it, I announced. "Fuck off," a boy replied. "Fuck off and shove the window up your ass."

I sulked.

I got a pail, a window mop, and started to wash it.

They watched me. How could anyone sit all day, as they had done up to that point, and do nothing but eat and listen to the radio? It did not occur to me then that there was nothing for them to do. Life had stopped for them long ago. They were waiting — for what, I didn't know. They didn't know. They were the white world's victims. No revolution had yet found a way to free them and give sense to their life. (How beautiful Bill L. and Joe T. are. They are addicts. The end is near, the grave breathes them in. They could be anything and do anything they wished if there were some way for them to embrace and desire life. But death is what they fondle, and I didn't know how to tear them away from death.)

I put up a sign in the window: anyone who wants to study math, history, art, music — anything — come in and ask me about it. I gathered books and furniture. An aunt died and left in storage a grand collection of oriental rugs, Chippendale chairs, and cloth-of-gold couches. I got them out and brought them to the storefront.

I asked Tim, a fifteen-year-old boy, who had the smile of an African chief I saw once in Arusha, if he'd help me build some bookcases. (I had called up every publisher I knew and asked for books. They came in by the hundreds.) "Why the fuck should I? No one ever did nothing for me. Why should I fuck around with fucking books for you? Anyway, I can't read." (To this day he is stalled in a treacherous world, this good, sad, and lost man.)

I had learned that in America a black man's sense of self and history is maimed by the memory of his life within a racist world. When I lived in Africa, I could talk with students about Sartre, Plato, Pierre Teilhard de Chardin, Joyce, and Shakespeare. I could not talk to them about their mythology. It was their mythology — I *think* — that gave them revolutionary wisdom; at least, it fed it with a force uncontaminated by "Western" feeling.

Nick, one of the "citizens" of the block, told me that when he was a boy he spent a good deal of his time in jail. When he came out, one of his teachers one day gave him a copy of *Life* magazine. In one vulgarized historical layout was an illustrated essay about Greek and Roman gods and heroes. Every book Nick remembered reading up until then seemed to him to be about Little Black Sambo. The discovery of the stories about Aeneas and Ulysses and their mythologies enchanted him. He wondered why the African tribesmen he saw in the movies always looked noble and grand in spite of their poverty and tattered clothes, in spite of their hunger and the burden of colonial rule. "Myth!" he shouted at me. "It was their mythology and communion with the world that saved them. Like Aeneas and

Ulysses, those tribes had a power that no general or king or capitalist could destroy. I believed from then on in the mythology of my people. It saved my life."

I wished I could have given Joe and Billy the *Aeneid* and the *Iliad*.

I told the kids I would give them classes in poetry. One afternoon, when they seemed less furious at me than usual, they came and sat around my aunt's Sheraton table to hear me talk about Wordsworth. I read them that section from *The Prelude* where Wordsworth "steals" a boat and rows out into the middle of a lake, late at night. The hills around the lake are transformed, by his fear and the darkness, into hulking mythological presences.

It reminded one boy of the day he robbed a drugstore. He was excited and frightened. "The motherfucking cops could come any minute and dump me in jail. But Jesus it was wonderful! He shook all over, the pig Jew I robbed. He nearly peed with fright. It was like a mystery story."

That was his way to read that poem. For an academic, this kind of reading might seem absurd. But I am convinced it is an intuition as accurate as any he might find in a scholarly journal.

Our library became, slowly, a place of books and wonder and, for these children, a beleaguered solitude. I hid the leaky pipes with a false ceiling. I was given fluorescent lights and threw away the twenty-five-foot extension cord we had hung one enormous bulb from, dragging it around like a torch in the shadows. I nailed a bamboo screen across the back wall and hung on it a map of the world and pictures of Africa, India, China, Egypt, Alaska, and any strange and distant place I came across in *National Geographic*. (That magazine is a dayspring for the children. They find the riddle of the world in it: the world's variety and wonder of "differences": the faces of Eskimos, Indians, Balinese, Japanese, Africans; their houses and their dress, their countrysides, their rituals. For these children, the world outside the city is as strange as if it were in another galaxy.)

The senses in Harlem suffer in a long, malevolent dark night. In that city of the dispossessed, ignored, despised, and forgotten by the powers, wounds never heal, noses run the year round, skin dries up, and children suffer from malnutrition and from a vicious kind of retardation that thrives on a bad diet.

I built our storefront into a place where the senses were freed from the fate of the streets.

I tried teaching the children to love the world; it is so easy to hate it in Harlem. I tried giving the children that sense of life that Camus says Sisyphus discovered when he returned to the earth for a time from the Underworld: "When he had seen again the face of this world, enjoyed water and sun, warm stones and the sea he no longer wanted to go back to the infernal darkness. . . . Many years more he lived facing the curve of the gulf, the sparkling sea and the smiles of earth."

13

Harlem (Continued)

I KNOW NOTHING OF HUNGER. Public hatred, private prejudice, have never touched my life. I have lived mostly in the midst of beauty. Harlem is part of the world in which I elected to work. I shall stay there as long as I have the strength and hope to remain, despite the fact that strength of spirit and hope are flayed rather horribly in Harlem's streets.

I have worked in Harlem for forty years. I came there in July 1966. I first worked as a volunteer in a poverty program for two months, went off to Israel, and returned in September to begin my task. About the nature of that task I knew nothing. I appeared one day on the street and began to build in half of a storefront on Madison Avenue between 128th and 129th Streets a library; in a few months I had collected about a thousand books for children and adults. (Marion Morehouse, e. e. cummings's widow, Robert Lowell, Robert Hutchins,

Richard Eberhart, Louise Bogan, Roger Straus, and dozens of other friends in publishing gave us great treasures from their own libraries. We had quite a wonderful, varied selection.)

It soon became clear that what I ought to start, however, and what seemed needed, was the establishment of a nursery for the very young. In September 1967, with the help of Tom Timmins, a friend of mine from the University of Notre Dame, I began the Children's Storefront School. First, there were five children, and over the years I moved the school from building to building along the avenue and down on 129th Street between Madison and Park. For the first year I also ran tutoring sessions for older children in the afternoons.

In 1973, a day after I had moved into a new building, a couple of transvestites had a quarrel on the top floor of the building, set fire to their apartment, and the flames that raged through it burned a hole in the roof. The next morning, I arrived to find my nursery destroyed. That happened in November, and for the next five months I went each day to Harlem in an effort to keep in touch with the children and with the vision of my work there, which overnight had been rather battered.

One evening in February of 1974, as I was preparing to shut down for the day, a beat-up old car drove up to the curb, and someone within called my name. The day had been a hellish one. The wreckage of the fire was still hanging on the facade of the building like briny weeds: charred wood, broken glass, fallen plaster. The streets were piled with garbage. The people moved along with extreme sadness, it seemed to me, but of course I was sad as well, filled with the hopelessness of everything about me. I wandered over and, peering into the car, I saw, sitting in the far corner, wrapped in a black mink coat, Queen Juliana of the Netherlands. Beside her in the back seat was her daughter Princess Christina, and a friend. In the front seat were three men: a chauffeur and two very frightened gentlemen with guns. I had met Princess Christina when I had traveled to Holland for the wedding of my friend Frank Houben. When Princess Christina came to live in New York City in the late 1960s, she volunteered as a music teacher in the Children's Storefront School. Though I knew her daughter well, I had never met the queen before that day. I think Christina wanted to show her mother the school where she worked. The queen was in town to announce the engagement of Princess Christina to my old friend Jorge Guillermo, who had been a trusted colleague at the Storefront School for almost three years. He was one of the few, white or black, who seemed to understand exactly what I was doing in Harlem.

I was a bit unnerved. But I thought, How marvelously comic; there in the midst of poverty, death, and violence, where the lamentation of the children burned hotter than any fire, was one of the world's richest women. The queen was a great lady, quite simple and direct, not given to the tremendous vanities of mythic queens. She offered to take me home, I squeezed myself in the back seat, and we headed downtown. The queen and I talked of human hope, of the power of the spirit, of the truths of religion and the mystery of God, and of the despair around us. At 115th Street and Park Avenue, under the elevated railroad track, the car stopped for a light. The queen said, "Ned, I think some-one is setting fire to that car." She pointed to a couple of fellows who were pouring something over the motor of an abandoned junk heap, something that increased the flames already shooting out of it. As we drove off, the car exploded in a great roar. "Your Majesty, that's Harlem: flame, fire, destruction," I said.

I had come to Harlem to work with the poor. While I had been preparing to teach in a college, it soon became clear to me that I did not want to traipse about, forever clutching English literature anthologies in my arms. I did not want to spend my life in academe. Harlem drew me. I followed my nose and landed there. I know that if I stayed in the United States, I would have to be involved in somehow changing it.

What I accomplished in Harlem has been very hard indeed, not the work in my school or the children, but the place: the spirit of the streets, the spiritual vi-sion of the inhabitants, the quality of hope, of love — or the lack of it, of celebration, the state of the family, the notion of childhood, the fabric of life. Those have tested me, often brutally.

Harlem is still a city within the city of New York, a colony within the nation of the United States. It shares a condition of misery with all the colonial states in this world, with the migrant communities within this land, with the Indian tribes on their reservations, with the little street urchins in Dublin. They all share a com-mon agony: the dominion of death over the forces of life in every aspect — in education, in the courts, in diet, in the markets, in hospitals, in prisons, in the very idea of citizenship that prevails in the constitutions of the lands in which these dispossessed live.

I have no sense, any longer, of color. No man is just black in my eyes and therefore something apart from his other dispossessed, oppressed brothers. Life is a gift the gods gave all men; intellect is; joy is; hope is; vision is. The agony of my children in Harlem is a shared agony; a hungry child in the back streets of Dublin is brother to a hungry, beaten child on 129th Street.

I see Harlem, I think, as clearly as anyone. It is a driven community. The streets are great barbed nets that capture the sensibilities of the people and relentlessly maul the will to survive. In the years that I have been here, I have seen the loveliest of children turn into animals. I have seen beautiful, caring women turn into passive mothers who transmit to their children the malignant despair that has bent their own lives out of shape.

You see, I think the cycle of poverty becomes almost a physical occurrence in the oppressed peoples. It establishes in the blood a weakness and a tendency to capitulate, just as in some families, mine for one, liquor lurks in the shadows to grab up the best of our minds and destroy them. I do not speak now of a genetic weakness, but of a psychic-imaginative one that captures the essence of the person and pushes it toward the abyss.

The most difficult thing is discovering how to bring change into a community where the very idea of change is alien. I have learned that it does not really mean very much to a man driven into the darkness of racial oppression to offer him a way out, since the way out demands an effort of will and imagination that is simply no longer within his spirit. My work is hard for that reason, perhaps for that reason alone. One cannot move a politically, spiritually, and imaginatively dead psyche, no matter how one tries, unless *within* the state, *within* the community, *within* the person, there is a simultaneous movement for change going on, however feeble and stricken that movement may be.

I call my schools liberation camps, for what I indeed seek to do is free children, at the earliest age, to the possibilities of growth, to stem the tide of that venomous despair that lays all hope to waste. The gradual, devastating encroachment on childhood of the forces of evil is terrible to watch. The forces that devastate children are lack of proper food; lack of proper rest; lack of proper medical attention; lack of curative psychiatric, spiritual, and parental care; and the lack, too, of an environment in which a child can explore, discover, and learn to love the world. For some children, life at home is an agony of Grecian proportions, but no Greek tragedy ever had such a terrible countryside in which to work out its agony. Our children are not buoyed up by any myth, and no visionary is ready to offer his sense of man as a balm to their wounds; no court, no poet, no prophet, is waiting for the moment to crush their oppressors.

The wreckage in Harlem is almost total, and the possibility for change now, as I write, some forty years later, is still questionable. All I was able to do then, and all I can do now, is prod, as best I can, the fires of life into flame in the youngest, in the hope of igniting in at least one child the fury and passion of revolution. I am always filled with hope, but that hope is tempered by the demons of oppression.

I think now, in these desperate thoughts, of Dreux. He was an angelic creature. Two years old, tiny but strong, with a smile that could crack, if any smile could, the marrow of tragedy. He was the tenth of eleven children, with the twelfth on the way. His mother was a gentle, gracious woman, utterly passive, proud, and dominated by a man who used her for his own wishes and abandoned her, letting her fend for herself.

From the chaos, Dreux came each day to our school, showering on all of us his glorious, gentle spirit. He spoke hardly a word but for gleeful signs and whispers of joy. I thought each day, again and again, of his future. What would happen to him when the twelfth child came? He would have to drop one step lower in the pecking order and learn, if he could, how to cope with a short ration, shorter than ever before (and it was always meager), of love.

The beginning of decay was already there, in one of the loveliest of children. The process within the mother had taken the form of extreme passivity, an almost sacral passivity, a giving-up that was clipping the wings of her children. It is thus, I noticed, with so many of our mothers. Time, the system, the world, sex, childbearing, death, sickness, the decay of the buildings that house them, all take their toll, rendering the victims silent and often luminously gentle.

Each day, I saw some new shape intrude on the beauty of Dreux; it took up residence in the interior places beyond his eyes, in his way of playing with his friends, in the emergence of a violent, undisciplined attitude toward learning. The change struck me like a bullet. Even his smile had been infected; his whole style seemed already askew, embittered, caged.

As are all the cities of the dispossessed, Harlem is in the vise grip of an insatiable cycle of poverty, a beast of many forms, as differing as the communities it inhabits, like a pestilence. It does no good to say that one is speaking of the victims of political oppression, racial hatred, religious unconcern, as if that can somehow make the horror less real. It does no good to mourn the evils of the past and seek political change, for such mourning is vain, and political change is unlikely. Harlem, as is true of all the cities of the dispossessed, is a completely apolitical community. No one there knows the first thing about his plight; no one knows what the politicians are doing, what they can do, what they are not doing. Elections come and go, nothing changes; no one rises up with any kind of energy to force change. Without a revolutionary change of vision within the nation itself, I do not think that anything will ever happen to transform the lives of the people I work with and love so dearly. Unless, of course, we can raise a generation of visionaries, unless the people themselves, through education and political enlightenment, shout "Enough!" and inflict a curing energy on their lives.

I am in Harlem to seek ways to bring to the children a sense of life and hope that they do not have; I work with fear and trembling toward the advent of that realization.

How strange it all is now. As I walk in Harlem and watch, my memory is crowded with the past and its encounters over many years with children, children, children. Not just my kidnapped child, but the others who did not have even my erratic care, my limited but utterly devoted attention to "being a parent." And no blame of parent or guardian casts even the slightest shadow over my thoughts, just horror, horror that a society such as this democratic one has failed so utterly, and continues to fail utterly, in its guardianship of the oppressed child.

They come to me, the children whose lives I recall, through the long passage of a blighted time, forty years on one block, nearly every day, during the long death of Ricky (it took him six years to die) and the long death of the lives that follow now.

14

Harlem Stories

*T*HE STORIES ARE HISTORIES OF SOME children I have known and loved and their families. The narrative is, alas, grim, but always touched by an elusive and real tragic grandeur.

What folly led me to think that I alone could stop the darkness from overtaking these beautiful children? For I know that no matter how I tried, unless what we began were taken up by the schools, survival would be impossible. What was before would continue into the future.

I want to stop the guardians of the children I watch each day from the stoop of my new school, stop them in their tracks as I see them screaming at their charges, walk ahead of them and leave them trudging behind, calling them "bad." A child hears everything, sees everything, remembers everything, forgets nothing, and the food you put into his mouth can kill.

I am fully aware, however, that I can do nothing to save them. That seems to be their lot. But I do believe that the schools they attend, the schools in the cities of the oppressed, should be manned by teachers learned in the skills of liberation, healing, patience, and hope. As the tribes of the unschooled grow, so does their anger, their despair. I see in the bodies, in the eyes, in the language of that tribe a baleful manner. I am often scared of them — scared not of what they can do to me, but of what they can do to each other, to their children, to the world around them.

I have been working for forty years on 129th Street, in the two schools I founded. How is it that the city, the state, the nation, have made no strides in bringing life and hope to that ravaged community? So little has changed. There is now a Starbucks on the corner of 125th and Lenox. Buildings are being renovated. Brownstones with bright new facades and superior kitchens fetch thousands a month in rent. Supermarkets spring up, and there is a new flash in the tree-lined streets. Is it all politics, public relations? I have sat on stoops these four decades, watching as the oppressed child moves up and down the streets with the same burden of despair growing each day more and more visible on tender little shoulders. Politicians, churches, Clinton flitting in and out of his Harlem office, the Board of Education and its manipulation of statistics and reading scores — nothing has brought new life to the oppressed.

*   *   *

Memory can be a place of suffocating ethers, especially if it has no bright spaces, no silence, no peace. The communities of the oppressed tend toward despair, and it is only their radiant faith in the final justice of the Almighty that makes life tolerable. Even now, in my new school, I am astonished by the immensity of sheer faith in divine goodness.

It does me no good in my work to forget the past, but rather it emboldens me to continue, for the children I knew in the past come to my sorties here and there in Harlem and in the world to remind me how little has changed.

My old school was once lodged in a building on East 129th Street. I had renovated the left apartment on the first floor. It was quite beautiful, and the children loved it. The building was owned by a local black church. In that building there were perhaps five families: a mother, Rasha, and her child Mighty Simon; Mrs. Littleforest and her grandniece Millicent; David Christopher, seventy, and Mrs. Hatbrightness, eighty. They lived in that building without heat in the bitter cold, without hot water, all contained in a fabric gnawed by rats, with urine spewing from rotten pipes, feces molding away in the cellar. A hole was burned in the roof during a fire that junkies had set, and water poured down for days into the apartments below. (A radiator with a hole in its casing shot out boiling steam over Mighty Simon one night as he slept. We took another radiator from an empty apartment and replaced it.)

Men, children, women, the illiterate, the infirm, lived embraced by that building's evil. For that evil they paid rent to the church.

During the hectic months of our renovation, I got into a terrible argument over our lease. We had propped up collapsing floors, repaired walls between apartments abutting ours, patched up plumbing in apartments above us. The church refused to give us help. They had the lock changed on our door, making it clear we'd not get back into an apartment into which we had sunk, for us, a fortune ($6,000) unless we signed a lease.

I went to the church office in a rage, into the office of the deaconess who managed the church's affairs, with a check for $500 in deposit and rent in my hand. She was dressed in a long red skirt, a flowered blouse, a red turban. Another woman sat beside her at the desk. She covered her face with her hand and said nothing. I gave the check to the manager; she handed me back a lease and a receipt.

"Where is the pastor?" I asked.

"He is out working. He is doing his Father's business," she said.

"What is his father's business?"

"God's business," she said, "that is what he is about."

There it all was: the rot of man, incarnate. I had no need ever to think again about my work in Harlem, whether I should stay, whether it was worth it. I knew then that the children I worked with were victims not merely of white racist power, but of black power, too. The deacon in his cassock, miter, and pointed hat, with the Bible in his greased hands, greased with the rent I was paying, the rents that other folk in my building were paying, greased with their cries in the night, with their chilled bones, with the rats and roaches, with the rains and winds that inhabited their dreams and waking hours — he appeared to me then like a colossal animal, sated with the body's pains and the soul's agony, preaching Jesus, salvation, and the goodness of God.

The Smiths lived in a building owned not by a church but by the city. It began well. The building was renovated with taste — elevators, security at the doors, garbage disposal chutes in the halls. But within a month it began to decay. The elevators broke down, the doors fell off their hinges, security vanished, and the garbage chutes were clogged.

The Smiths — Berta, Lindy, Tim, Randy, Lilly, Mike, and Amos — came to it in tatters. Berta, the mother, was a drunkard. She hoarded her monthly check for booze and clothes and the upkeep on a car. The children settled into the apartment as if it were a swamp of quicksand. I'd visit and watch the children fall into the grip of that vacuum. Little Amos, most of all, a quiet kid when he came to our school, was growing mute and finally lost all coherence in his speech. I lost sight of him for a few months, and then on a cold midwinter day, I saw him wandering the streets in light trousers and a summer shirt, no socks, no underwear.

"Where are you going?" I asked him. "Nowhere? Are you hungry?"

"Yes."

"Did you have breakfast?"

"No."

"Did any of your brothers and sisters have breakfast?"

"No."

We went back to his apartment. The place was ravaged. There had been a fight in the flat some months before, I was told by Berta's sister, and the place was burned out. The stink of charred cloth and wood and plaster lingered, but no one had moved out. Everything had stayed: kin, friends, enemies, boyfriends, girlfriends, roaches, liquor bottles. The family had been ordered out but had not moved. (The mills of eviction grind slow.)

Meanwhile, the mother continued her own wandering. She was fed well, slept soundly, dressed warmly, and drove a car, while the children rotted. His mother insisted Amos was retarded. But he wasn't retarded when he came to my school. He had been frozen to the grid of his few square feet of charred space. In a sense, his house became him; he became his house. He went willy-nilly to school. But it did him no good; in fact it injured him. Whatever the school could muster in energy, patience, and sheer hard-nosed intellectual bullying was lost utterly when Amos returned home.

That house was a prison. Most people I talk to about my work in Harlem cannot imagine that what I say about the homes of our children is true. Why don't "they" clean their damn places up? Cleaning up has to do with cleaning up schools, streets, plumbing, courts, politicians, cops, junkies, pimps, muggers, storekeepers, landlords. What Amos was shoved into was not merely a badly kept household; it was an oppressed, brutalized universe. When he walked through the streets in midwinter with no socks or undershirt, he was not merely walking out of a house where someone forgot to dress him; he was walking out of a universe where his life, his survival, were matters no one cared a damn about.

The social services came and went in all their guises — welfare caseworkers, inspectors, nuns, O'Gorman, irate neighbors — nothing ever happened that changed Amos Smith's family. The immensity of moving six children out of hell into an anteroom of survival was too much of a task for those who would have moved them if they could.

Amos, his mother, his sisters and brothers, have finally been relocated. I do not know where they are, but I do know it will be the same as it has been in every other place they have lived. And it will, alas, continue to be so. The event that moved them away from that burned-out husk was a wild drive through the Harlem streets late at night, five children in the car, a drunken mother at the wheel. She careened into a lamppost, tossing an old gentleman who happened to be crossing in front of her high in the air. He did not die, but his legs and arms were shattered. The children were dumped in a shelter for a day and then given back to Berta. And life went on for them as before.

*   *   *

Diane Arbus was a great photographer. Her vision reminds me of the work of Flannery O'Connor. She could with her genius, as Flannery could, transform the grotesque into a vision of cumbersome, wrecked grace. She came to photograph me for *Vogue*, and spent the entire day trying to get something of me into her camera. She stood me on snowdrifts, in backyards, in dark alleys; she dressed me in Aran sweaters, overalls, turtlenecks, but could not seem to connect her camera with O'Gorman's spirit. (I would loved to have seen those photos — I never did. I am sure she must have gotten a bit of the grotesque in me!) We walked a lot during that day, and along the way visited Donald and his mother, Lucienne.

Donald was the first child I really got to know in Harlem. He was two when I first saw him. It was a chilly day, early autumn, as I walked up the stairs. And there he sat: two years old, skinny, silent, huddled on a bed in his undershorts, thumb in his mouth, his other hand holding his earlobe. Ruby, his paternal grandmother, was a great lady, I discovered as I grew to know her, sat in her little bedroom next to the living room, ill but vigilant, wise, compassionate, as the world around her tumbled down.

I saw Donald every day. I took him for walks, visited friends with him, took him to the country, and finally, after weeks, he began to talk and smile. I was a neophyte in the world of Harlem then, and didn't notice that my attentions got on the nerves of his family. They locked him in the apartment and would not let me see him for weeks. I think I was the first man, white

or otherwise, ever to challenge their power of dominion over their child.

Donald had a brother, Jeremiah — lame, retarded,
half blind — who reeled around the apartment like a
top gone berserk. He flung himself on the floor, crashed
into walls, reached with his claw hands out to anything
that would hold him and caress him. That was Ruby's
work. Donald's father came each day or so to make love
to his mother and beat her up. He was an addict, a
pusher, and a vicious, brutal man. Donald's mother, Lucienne, got into drugs and brought her lesbian lover
home with her, often with an extra girl. I saw roaches
nestled in a stick of butter in Donald's apartment.

Ruby was dying. Her heart was weak, and she had
cancer. But it was her mediation with the family that
let Donald's mother allow him to see me again. When
Ruby died, the family split up. Donald's mother got
deeper into drugs and sex, flitted into one apartment
after another, each worse than the one before. I finally
tracked them down to a foul hole on 123rd Street. The
stairs to the flat were crowded with addicts shoving
in needles. The streets were filled with transvestites,
whores, pimps, and pushers. Donald never left his apartment but for an occasional excursion to school. By then
he had a baby sister, and the three children, the mother,
and her pals all lived in holy terror until one day Jeremiah woke up with a dead junkie beside him in bed.
Then the authorities came, took away the children, and
placed them in new homes.

Their caseworkers moved them into inadequate
homes. The children were miserable, and after a while

Lucienne rehabilitated herself enough to please the overworked social worker, and the children, except for Jeremiah, came back to the mother! And to the lesbian girlfriends, the liquor, the sex, the dope.

I wrote of the photo Diane Arbus took of Donald and his mother. They are both sitting on a beaten-up old bed; the linen is ripped and soiled. Behind them is a wall of cracked plaster; on the floor, torn soiled linoleum. Donald and his mother stare into the camera, void of response — blank, sullen, tired.

Why was he lost? Why were the beginnings of his new life cut off before they had a chance to grow? Why did his mother have such power of persuasion over courts and social workers, power strong enough to get her child back into her custody? She told me again and again during her children's absence that she was working to get them back. But what kind of work was she doing? She got an apartment in the Bronx, hustled furniture for it, got stricken off welfare for fooling with her welfare check, and found the city agencies were so overworked that they simply let the children go. She left the Bronx and moved into an apartment not far from my nursery. Donald, now in the fifth grade, roamed, hungry, in tatters, claws out at the world for some sign that it was not going to destroy him. I knew that it would.

The family is a complicated unit to deal with in the best of worlds. If it works well, a family serves as a landscape in which a child can grow, learn of the world, love it, manage it well for his good and for the good of others. In that family, when he is born, a child must receive food, sleep, understanding, and those multitudinous signs of affection and hope that build the strong ground a happy, successful man will spring from. If the family, in all its parts, is decaying, the child will not survive unless he is possessed by a strong creative demon and by a strong environment outside the family.

One afternoon, as I was shutting down my new school for the day, suddenly there in the classroom stood a young man, six feet tall, terribly overweight, silent, his eyes vacant and his spirit frayed. It was Donald. "How are you?" I said. He answered that he had a child who lived with its mother, that he had no job, and I saw then, in a shock of brutal intensity, that there before me was a victim. Nothing I had done for him in the past, nothing I had wished for his life, had occurred; he would die a victim, so brutal the past, so reckless the forms of oppression that had crippled that sweet little body I had so often carried in my arms to school.

The children of the oppressed suffer the year through with minor irritations of all kinds. It seems their noses run in all seasons. Their skin is always dry. They are laid up again and again with strange colds, often medicated with strong doses of penicillin when I know all they really need is bed rest, orange juice, a warm pillow, sleep, and love. Earaches, eye infections, stomachaches, vomiting, general malaise, malinger in the bodies of the little ones, breaking down their spirit, lowering their resistance, generally ruining the bodies they must carry with them to the grave.

When I ask what kind of medication they are giving their children, the mothers inevitably answer "antibiotics," or over-the-counter remedies that I cannot recall ever curing anything. The medication is sometimes taken for months, and nothing is cured.

A child born into destitution must have easy access to the healing process in all its variety. Begin with clinics for mothers of unborn children. A mother of an unborn child needs, imperatively, attention paid to the state of her body, to its nutrition, and to its health during the nine months her child is carried within her. Nutritional guidance at a clinic is of little use, since there is no way to make certain that it will be followed; there may not even be food in the house of the kind recommended at the clinic. The "ideal" (and, I fear, unreal) vision I propose is the establishment, say, every ten blocks of nutritional clinics that can offer on-the-spot guidance to mothers, who have not the foggiest notion of what healthy food is. The snag in this projected decentralized "welfare system" is the follow-up. Democracy permits little tolerance for interference in the mode of family living, whether or not that mode destroys life. Mothers must learn and be convinced that what they are doing is destroying their children.

Staffed partly by community people and partly by city workers, such clinics would be easy enough to set up. The rubble of old houses in various states of decay in our community — some beyond help or renovation, but others still recoverable — would supply the space in a short time. One would need only a stove, an icebox, dry milk, basic vitamins, a supply of fresh fruit, vegetables, cheeses, simple food high in protein that would either be given out to mothers or used as examples of what they should buy at the market. This vision of mine, this "sense of crisis," is often alien in the dispossessed. Folks on the edge must be convinced; an expectant mother must feel at the core of her being that if she imposes a bad diet upon the child she carries through another pregnancy, that child will suffer and will probably be born deficient.

At four, Dillie was already heading toward failure. Dillie lived in a captive world, walled in on all sides by the conventions of her past. Her mother was a strange, sullen woman who in occasional fits of geniality could be quite lovely, but these moments were few. For the most part, the mother could not communicate a thought or a feeling to Dillie, a silent creature with a ravishing smile that had no echo in her eyes or in her actions. Trapped in her house, Dillie often spent long hours alone with her sister. It would have taken an event of epochal force to rescue her from her mother.

    I knew her for two years. When I had to temporarily shut down my school (the ceiling had collapsed, the phone went dead, and the electricity was cut off), I lost touch with Dillie. She disappeared into the rain and snows of winter, into its terminal dark and freezing loneliness. She emerged in early summer, stumbling out, frayed, it seemed, from a long captivity in darkness.

"Hello, Lilly," I called, using the nickname her mother gave her when she first told me the child's name. The little girl said nothing. But her smile, that mask of her agony, flooded her face.

"Come here," I said. She ran to me. She would have run to any friendly creature. When I lifted her up, I lifted not a child but a puppet, a thing moved not by life but by forces in an alien universe. I knew that as long as she was in the captivity of her mother, whatever ailed her, whatever sickness she might be possessed by, genetic or intellectual, as long as that captivity lasted, Dillie's chances of conquering the evils around her were poor.

There is a fortresslike aloofness about Harlem's buildings. These buildings have a way of penetrating into the lives of the folk who live there, communicating their decay to the inhabitants as a jail might to a prisoner. Dillie's building was hard to get into. The front door was locked; the door that led from the little entryway beyond it into the hall was double-locked, padlocks and all. Most of my children are accessible to me, but Dillie was hidden away. She could be locked in there for months, and I'd never get to see her unless my shouts were heard five flights up by her mother, or unless the superintendent, as a favor, climbed to her apartment to see what was going on.

"There's a rainfall of roaches, spiders, beetles, and crap in the mornin', Ned. Help me," her mother cried once in despair. Floors collapse, roofs split open under the pressure of rainwater, yet in the midst of it all the family sits, continuing its life, the children in rubble like shattered pieces of furniture.

When Dillie came to us, I tried everything I could to move her to respond to me and to the world. I teased her, tickled her, in an effort to make her aware of the outside world. I sat with her and pointed to objects, the simplest — dogs, streets, cars, buildings — asking her to repeat their names after me. She remained silent; her little body could not connect with anything.

Another little girl, eight years old, walked about like an overwound clock, ready to spring any minute into fragments. Like Dillie, she could not contact the world beyond her because she simply had no skills to make that connection. She learned nothing in school. Her speech was the mirror of her inner life, incoherent, garbled. She spoke in the manner she had learned from her kin, who were illiterate, drunken, and unresponsive to her needs. When I spoke to some black folk about her speech, they said it was her birthright. That was just one myth among many people believed about their lives, and transmitted to their children, and their children to their children. Soon it became dogma.

The greatest myth, of course, is that a dysfunctional family is better than no family; that a mother, no matter how she bends children into grotesque beings, is better than no mother; that living with your kin, no matter the inherited sickness of the oppressed, is better than no kin; that a language, part of your heritage, never mind that no one understands you when you speak, is a good language and ought to be perpetuated.

I hope the first myth that my work in Harlem will shatter is that possession of a child is nine-tenths of the law and that blood ties, no matter how malign, are better than no ties.

Dillie's mother controlled her child as severely and brutally as a slave master did a slave. Such violations of that little girl's rights to life and growth are a crime and must be seen as such. I am encouraged by the action of a San Bernadino, California, court regarding a woman whose twins were born with heroin withdrawal symptoms. The authorities said the mother had been warned several times by a welfare department nurse that heroin addiction could endanger her unborn children; they filed felony child abuse charges against her, and the care of the infants was given to her sister.

Dillie's mother was a gentle woman who could not smile. I never heard her say, nor did I see her do, one thing that would indicate to me that life meant much to her. I felt often that if she fell into a fissure in the earth, I'd hear not a sound from her as she plummeted to her death. Her voice was a monotone, no inflection. She spoke to me in the wandering, disconnected style that is the keening of the dispossessed as they roam the blasted earth.

One mother came to me and whispered, "He is dead, my man, he is dead." I was sorry, I said, thinking he had just died. I asked when it happened. "In May," she said. That was five months before. And such a world of no beginning, no middle, no end was the world Dillie lived in. A world undefined, horizonless, mute.

15

The Sensibility of Misery

SOMEWHERE IN HIS NOTEBOOKS, CAMUS WRITES, "A certain number of years lived in misery are sufficient to construct a sensibility."

This sensibility of misery is not merely transmitted helter-skelter to the children who come to our school. It is a legacy of long standing in the families they come from; it is a blighted birthright, a malign inheritance, a curse visited by the demons of history, and it gets into the blood. It is both tough and tragic to inquire into the reasons for the destruction of a child, for it means we must tread on very inhospitable ground, travel to places where mysteries of history and inheritance come somehow into shadowed play.

We all inherit our world, good and bad, beautiful and ugly, filled with horror, romance, sex, loneliness, fear, peace, wisdom, doltishness. We come from our ancestors and from our place on the earth — this street, that village, those hills, that burrow, that jail, that mountaintop, that stinking hole. Into each of our lives the whole prism of our mystery falls.

What I have learned of children in Harlem, I learned first of all because I knew it about myself.

I was introduced to the sensibility of misery. But it was a misery of the nerves, of the affections. I accuse no one in my family, neither my parents nor my ancestors, for that misery emanated from having grown up in a broken home. It was there in me like a seed ready to burst into flower given the right season, the efficient spiritual squall or malicious imp; it was there, ready to overwhelm me, as such seeds of despair and sickness can overwhelm all men. But in my life certain safeguards were in constant attendance on my growth — genial spirits in many guises, in every kind of strange visitation, in the very walls and floors, kitchens and gardens, of my childhood.

My parents were beautiful children of the 1920s and '30s. They danced their way through life, riding horses, sailing, drinking, and I remember nothing more beautiful than watching them leave for the hunt club in their evening clothes as I looked from my bedroom window fronting the harbor in Southport, my home for the first ten years of my childhood. To me they seemed always to be in flight from this world, a world that was collapsing all about them. For the great and terrible World War II was looming over them, and their golden youth was crumbling into the dust of time. When I looked at my mother then, I saw in her the great strength that saved her children from the holocaust of the end of her marriage, a strength that came from the beauty of the world she had known. She and my father both grew up with style, tradition, beauty, and those human feelings, described finally as "reverence for life," that ultimately save us all.

The differences between the oppressed and the unoppressed are obviously infinite. The crucial difference for me had to do with the atmosphere I breathed, with the things I saw, with the silence I learned to love, with the sweetness of clean sheets, regular meals, celebrations, journeys, and that sense of safety, of being preserved from the malice of the world. My will to survive — nay, more than survive, to flourish, to succeed, to have visions and to pursue them — was honored in those early years. It had little to do with my learning to read and do numbers by six. I was bad at learning, simply had a lazy streak, a kind of errant sensibility that got me into trouble, but that plateau of my spirit — that place in me where resided the strengths of will, imagination, hope, a nose for the good, and a repulsion for evil — that place was doing well.

A child's growth has only partially to do with what he learns. Child abuse has many faces. One is the physical battering of the child's body, and I've seen enough of that to make me despair, but there is another battering, one less easy to detect, difficult to bring to court, and easily hidden by parents. Observers of a child abused *within* cannot see it at all.

The sensibility of misery I knew little of, could know nothing of, since when I did fall into sadness, the armies of miracle-working powers in my spirit always came to the rescue. But they might not, had they not been carefully instilled into my spirit when I was young.

We simply *must* survive, no matter how much our parents connive against us to make survival difficult. We simply must survive, no matter how much governments connive against us to make that survival almost impossible. The education of the oppressed child is a desperate, lifesaving process, a fending off of devils.

American education has yet to begin to understand what it must offer the children of the oppressed. It is absurd to think that a child brought up under the conditions I am describing in this book can enter the traditional educational system and not be profoundly injured by it. The children who come to my school need skills of survival as much as they need skills of reading, writing, and arithmetic. They must be taught, at the very beginning, how to interpret their surroundings, things as basic as how to repair a furnace, how to seek help in emergencies, how to do simple carpentry so that a wreck of an apartment can be made a fortress against the elements. They must learn skills such as plastering, rudimentary plumbing, even cooking. And they must be taught history, *their* history — not African history, but the history of their lives. They must be taught to understand their plight and to question why they and their families are where they are.

What a child of the oppressed lacks most is not merely the physical and spiritual conditions for growth, but also protection from the suffering that ensues from deprivations. (In my childhood our attic was a haven for cousins and uncles and aunts who had to find refuge from the oppressions of liquor, desertion, bankruptcy. My father opened our house so that his kin who suffered could come to him for shelter.) For the children of the oppressed no such refuge exists. The schools, which ought to be a refuge for such children, are not.

What we must seek is a way to detect the presence of the forces of destruction that are crippling the innocent. Then we must discover ways to aid the child, so that that child's will to live is heard and heeded.

16

The Person of Fear

O N THE NIGHT MARTIN LUTHER KING JR. WAS ASSASSI-nated, I was in a bar in Greenwich Village, reading Thomas Hardy. I had spoken that night to my mother, who begged me not to go to Harlem the next morning. I told her that I would go, that I had to go, for if I did not, I would betray my faith in the children. I would be safe, I reassured her. No one would kill me.

And in the morning I went. The streets were empty. No children came. I opened the door to my little storefront school, and after putting some music on the phonograph, went outside and sat on a railing that separated the school from a grocery store. It was about nine o'clock. I sat there for the entire day, walking about the sidewalk, fetching coffee from the grocery, making some phone calls. I wanted whoever condemned white folks to see at least one who would not hide, would not cower in fear. It was, of course, a foolish act, an arrogant one, an act that could have harmed me, but nothing would keep me from my resolve to test my pacifist soul in the present fire.

Yet then, as now, Harlem was encased in a caul of violence. Years of life in the turbulence of racism had warped sensibilities, and the presence of a white man such as I was, afflicted with airs of energy and the innocent wish "to work there," broke speculation. I was as exposed as fire in dry straw. There was a certain lunacy in blundering into a landscape I knew so little about. My first day in Harlem was as my first day in Rome had been, a vista of a terra incognita. I really had no idea of where I was: north, east, south, west, it was all the same, a vast crumbling place with neither a familiar face nor a familiar landmark. When I finally settled down in my shattered little storefront on Madison Avenue and began inviting children in through my splintered door, I had no idea that I had stirred anger and a barbed bewilderment in a man I shall name the Person of Fear.

He came to me in the weeds of despair. He hung between high and stylish intelligence — he was a poet and musician — and swaggering fury. He stood there with fixed and rigid intensity. He watched me. He counted me up. He fixed me in his dreams. He took me into his nerves and fed upon my white body.

My schoolhouse, dilapidated as it was, was a white man's work. It was maintained by white money, white friends, despite the fact that the staff was nearly, by then, all black.

Someone had threatened to bomb the library if I didn't get out. The school closed. I stayed. The Person of Fear walked up and down the sidewalk, smiling and shaking his finger at me. I walked over to him on a rainy day when I was ready to cry out in rage and fear, put my head on his shoulder, and told him he was my brother. He laid his hand on me, rocked back on his feet, and laughed like a hill breathing fire.

The Person of Fear was an alien to his own people. He said he'd give free music lessons. There were no takers. The people were frightened by his fury, his hobnailed intelligence, and his prophetic stance.

On an afternoon when I was alone, and the children were out on a trip in the city, he came in and sat in the library with a friend. The Person of Fear held a cane decorated with pieces of colored glass and stone. His companion, a short, stocky boy with dark glasses, sat on the windowsill.

When I walked into the library to greet him, he whispered with cold languor, "Get him now." His friend leapt on me. He knocked me down and beat me on my back, head, spine, and kidneys. I ran from him, shouting for help. He thudded against my body like a tidal wave, spitting and biting, scratching and tearing into me as if I were Beelzebub. I protected my face for fear he'd scar me. I got free now and then and knocked over tables and chairs to trip him.

The Person of Fear followed him around. "Get him. Harder. Get his balls. Kick, kick, kick his balls until they fall off." I lifted up the phonograph and heaved it at him. I missed, and he was on me when he heard a police siren. He stopped, but the Person of Fear took his cane and drew a sword from it. He came toward me. This was it —

I would die. I grabbed an empty Coke bottle. I thought I'd smash it and drive the jagged end into his eyes.

I was a pacifist, but not until then did I know what it meant to be nonviolent when a man wanted to do me in. I prayed as he beat me that I'd not *wish* to hurt him. I decided, with uncharacteristic cool, not to touch him and swore, there on the floor, that if I ever lifted a hand to anyone in Harlem out of rage and hate, I'd leave Harlem for good. In the midst of this interior dialogue, I looked up and saw the Person of Fear straddling my chest, his sword pointed straight at my heart. I said to myself, "Okay, Lord" — and just when I thought I'd feel the blade ripping through me, the police drove up, and he ran off into the crowd outside and disappeared.

The children returned. I had straightened up the room, set some books and crayons on a table, and put a record on the phonograph (it did not break when I threw it).

Andy Harrell, though, knew something was wrong, and said, "Ned, I want to draw something. Give me black paper and crayons." When I was ready to lock the library for the night, Andy came and gave me his drawing. On the black paper he had drawn a field of yellow grass, and shooting up out of the black paper, transformed in his drawing into the world, was an enormous yellow flower. "It is a yellow flower, Ned, for you." That was Andy's sign of life to me.

The community was in an uproar. A meeting was called so that everyone would know what had happened and why it had happened. I had become a threat to the children. ("Maybe he'll come with a gun and kill the kids.") "Press charges," they demanded. I said no.

The Person of Fear had returned the morning of the meeting, carrying what some people on the street feared was a gun. He called me and the men from the block who had come to guard the storefront "faggots."

Horace said, "When he calls us faggots, he insults us. He may get one of us with that gun. If he does, we'll kill him. If we get hurt because you won't press charges, you'll be to blame."

I pressed charges.

It was all a matter of how one learned about the world. I had never defended myself against anyone. My world defended me. No law, good or bad, affected my life. I lived outside the law. A black man knows the law is of no use to him. The police, government, schools, armies, wars, are for the white man — for his good, his freedom, his advancement. A black man gets what the white man wants to give him. I was a pacifist and believed in nonviolence, because I had learned that peace was good and violence evil. In Harlem, life and the world is enemy. It must have sounded bizarre to the men who had been so good to me when I was in danger to hear me talk about nonviolence, turning the other cheek, and the other luxurious possibilities of a white man's world and philosophy.

17

A Possible Solution

*T*HE WELFARE SYSTEM'S TRAGEDY HAS TO DO WITH ITS size. There is simply not enough of anything to get it right, to get it to do its business effectively. I have watched it go its cumbersome, destructive way now for more than four decades. It cannot work, because there are simply too many children and parents and families with desperate needs who converge on its offices every day with problems of life and torment, death and illness.

As I have mentioned time and again, only if the system is decentralized, broken down into small community clinics, open twenty-four hours a day, will there be a change. For a family on welfare, the pitfalls increase, not because the family is unwilling to seek change but because the "system" is clotted with an almost hopelessly bureaucratic sensibility. To get from point A to point B is to run the gamut of filing cases, misplaced papers, angry and overworked social workers, and simple bread-and-butter disorganization. For a child with an earache, for a family with a hole in their ceiling, for a family facing eviction, the labor of finding medicine, plaster, and lodging simply, finally for many, runs into a distressed resignation, and nothing happens; enervating despair gets hold, and one stops trying to find a solution.

This utopic decentralization is a task not easily accomplished, I know, in a welfare system dependent for its existence on gathering everything into one place.

The decentralization of the institution of welfare in all its immense, paralyzing bulk would bring the issue of survival down to the streets. There, in small clinics, parents, a family, even the child itself, could come for healing in a time of illness or despair. The process would be immediate, kind, personal, yet vigilant and stern. I remember one girl who had to wait months for a proper diagnosis of a problem with one of her breasts. None of the journeys back and forth to clinics resulted in proper diagnosis. The child is well now, thanks to clinics outside "the system." Hundreds of other children are not as lucky, and disease continues its dreadful progress unabated. The banks, the city, now in my community renovate building after building for housing, while the welfare system creaks, stumbles, and fails. If the city could only build a local clinic in every building they renovate, and in every renovated building a mini school, a library, a garden, things would improve instantly. When asked whether Harlem has changed in the forty years of my labors there, I reply that although buildings are being restored, children and families of the oppressed still malinger in increasing poverty, in failed schools, and in disastrous welfare.

The problem is getting the loose ends of our children's lives hitched together. The system as it works now is best described, I think, as an enormous valley crossed by a thin rope bridge. On one side of the valley is water, food, healing oils, the friendly hearth, hope. To cross over is a nerve-shattering journey; one steps alone or with one's child over the howling abyss and its depths. Once there, one fetches provender and returns with just enough, or not quite enough, and nothing has changed; the homeland is still wasted, the day still at the mercy of the demons. One must set out each morning to seek salvation, and soon the journey is no longer possible for many. They become dead within; the healing on the other side of the chasm is not sufficient to undo the evil of the day.

That is the way I see the lives of our people in relation to the city, the churches, the state, the nation, all of their proclaimed healers. There is no healing whatsoever in Harlem's streets and its cavernous landscapes. The poor and their children must work at their own salvation. The day-to-day running of their lives never seems to have healing contact with the other side of the chasm.

The mini clinics I keep hoping for would act as life rafts for the wandering sick, for the weak child, the despairing family. They would offer simple healing, preventing the onslaught of major collapse of the body and spirit. We have witnessed with horror how the poor, in their diaspora after the hurricanes in New Orleans, were treated. If a similar disaster were to strike New York City, we would see the same abandonment of the poor.

My job in Harlem has been to bring to my schools a sense of the fruitful life.

Food on time, good, nourishing food; sleep, plenty of it, on clean sheets and with a bit of peace and order accompanying the process; a good education — that is, learning to read, write, add, etc., and to love the beautiful and shun evil; these constitute a proper and fruitful life for a child. The great revelation of growing up is when one begins to believe that of all gifts, life is the most precious. It is being able to think well of oneself and to believe that hidden in one's heart and in the world is the key to glory, success.

Black children know more about life by the age of two than most white children know at fifteen. They know about life, death, sex, love, growth, decay, and joy with an intensity and canniness that astonish and often frighten their teachers.

I delight in this canniness and intensity.

Harlem is a great city. It possesses a mammoth energy and indestructible life. It reminds me of the villages along the coast of Asia Minor, of the mountains of Maktar in Tunisia, of Casablanca, of the tribal villages in Tanzania. The black man in Harlem has inherited a tradition of music, ritual, hope, and often religious vision that is stylish and brilliantly *human*.

The worst thing that could happen in New York

City would be the disappearance of Harlem. While Harlem must be transformed physically, and crime and addiction must be destroyed, the place must endure. Harlem is the authentic village in the city of massed vulgarity, where people still retain the authentic gusto of life.

The goal of all healing in the cities of the dispossessed is to nurture and heal the body and liberate the mind. Only then is it possible to will a good and fruitful life.

I have worked a long time in Harlem. I have lost all hope in politicians, religion, courts, police, educators. The whole lot of the powerful have failed the poor, and continue to fail them. Only here and there, in my two schools, in some classroom with a heroic teacher, in a church with a heroic pastor, in a household with a heroic parent or guardian, only in those isolated campgrounds of change have I sensed that the oppressed, the dispossessed in this land, have a chance of life.

And the children have been there always, always, watching me as I get out of the car in the morning, sit on the stoop, open my arms to them, listen to them, deliver up to them the small gifts of our ramshackle school.

18

Last Trip to Rome

*M*Y SON RICK SAID, "When I die, Pop, I want three things: a party after mass, and my ashes scattered in Southport Harbor and then in the Vatican Gardens." I said okay. On January 24, 1996, he did. He had AIDS. We talked about his death and planned his going forth as we ate lunch at the Tex-Mex restaurant where he had worked before his torment broke him.

Rick loved Rome. When I first took him there, he was eight. I feared he might find Rome dull. I took him to dinner at Maestrostefano on the Piazza Navona and awaited his first reflection. It was raining, and the sky was silver and bright with that omnipresent Roman light. He ate his risotto with saffron and looked up at me and said, "Oh, Pop, it's so beautiful, like a silver dime in the sun!"

I packed a little box of his ashes, a dollop of them,

into the side pocket of an L. L. Bean canvas sack and covered it with a sock to act as ballast. I feared I would be found out, because someone had told me that it was not proper, illegal even, to transport ashes into foreign lands. Might they show up in customs as a forbidden substance? Most of Rick's ashes were taken by his brothers to his mother's grave. I had bought two small Indian papier-mâché boxes painted with bright imaginary flowers for the little I had the undertaker keep for me. The first box went into Southport Harbor. And with that second box, I headed toward Rome.

I have been visiting Rome for over forty years. It was in its massive, rudimentary glory when I arrived on Wednesday of Holy Week. The air was cold. The sun, like a great wildflower, leaned from the sky, hot and restless in the early spring. I was devoured by the city, by its difficulty, by its mystery, by its strange, aloof, ripe arrogance. I ventured out on Holy Thursday morning with Ricky's ashes in my pocket. The little pilgrimage had begun its final stage.

How was I to get into the Vatican Gardens? I had called one highly placed monsignor, and he said, quite briskly, that those gardens were the pope's. He walked in them. I could not. So I proceeded to inch my way up an umbrella pine that grew out of a terrace that lay in the shadow of St. Peter's dome and in view of the papal gardens. I unpacked the box carefully and quickly scattered part of the ashes around the base of the tree among small white flowers — a circle of pale gray bits. The rain announced for that evening would wash the ashes into the loam. Those that were left, I slipped into the Bernini fountain, the one on the right as you look toward the basilica. They swirled in the eddies, turning them dark for an instant, and then became lost in the waters that tumbled from the crown of the fountain, sucked into the Roman light that cannot vanish even under the darkest clouds. I washed out the box, closed it, and tossed it in the Tiber, where it would push on toward the Mediterranean.

I had given my son to the Roman deities, to their whims, to their sullen ways, to their madness, to their flesh and ruins, to all my memories.

In the Church of Santa Maria in Trastevere, for a couple of hundred lira, a spotlight will illuminate the mosaics over the main altar. One can see them for a few minutes in detail — bright, sparkling, intensely clear — but when the paid-for light goes out, the mosaics shine much brighter, their inner fire spinning through the dark, the fire hidden in the tesserae, in the holiness of the place. Like the view of St. Peter's from the Quirinale the morning I flew from Rome — the heavenly city, the mortal city, the glory of the world shining through the rose light, magnifying the horizon, giving it perspective after perspective — so it was with me and my recollections of my son. He had died, but he was alive and well somewhere in the kingdom, reflected so gloriously in the sacred landscapes of Rome where life suddenly, for me, flowered, announcing robustly the endurance of glory, the endurance of breath.*

---

* **Why I Was Fired from the Children's Storefront School.**
In July of 1998, the board of trustees fired me as headmaster of the Children's Storefront School. I was becoming intolerable. I would allow no one to impose order on my vision, which, I think, had gotten a bit ragged. I had "done whatever I pleased," from establishing courses in Latin and Greek to building an infrastructure that delighted my sense of what education ought to be in Harlem: a pedagogy of liberation, healing, classical studies, and a sort of freewheeling attitude in matters academic. I behaved badly for a week, and rented, that same July, the garden apartment of our present school. In December of 1998, eight children came to our first kindergarten: Nico (now at the Cathedral School), Jeannette, Mateo (now at the Caedmon), Idris (at Bank Street), Jamie Lee (at Manhattan Country Day School), Jalel, Qays, and Kiné (at St. Aloysius). I worked alone with some volunteers, and seven years later we have thirty children. We are supported by friends, and it is hard to make it all work.

Our pedagogy, rooted in Paolo Friere's seminal text *The Pedagogy of the Oppressed*, brings a great bounty of "texts": Chinese, Spanish, Latin, French, music, drama, dance, and a rigorous discipline in reading, math, history, geography, and the most difficult of all disciplines, joy.

We are not a white school or a black school, a Western civilization school or an Eastern civilization school. We are a school. Our children come from everywhere: from the middle class, from interracial families, from the very poor; our children are all mixed in the hurly-burly of many academic excellences, academic troubles, and throughout the day, music and laughter, peace and good food and conversation, are strong enough to wipe out all bureaucratic, institutional high-mindedness and the array of preconceptions that still govern the education of the oppressed.

19

A Gathering Up

W HAT, THEN, HAVE I DONE OVER THE LONG PASSAGE
of my life with children in Harlem, New York? I must
account somehow for these four decades. Have they
been years wasted in fierce combat with a city that
will not enter with salvic vision the tormented lives of
the oppressed child in its midst? Have they been just
the vainglorious efforts of a lonely man to seek meaning for a rather desperate life, a task to fill the rasping spaces of his loneliness? My life on 129th Street
seems such a splintered one, unavailable to simple
judgments of failure or success. I began when I was
thirty-five, and will leave that prophetic, bewildering,
holy landscape when I am seventy-six. But surely
something did happen to the children who came to me.
But what? What did they bring away with them from
their life with me and my colleagues in the Children's

Storefront School and the Ricardo O'Gorman Garden and School?

This is what I think I have done: I presented the world, its beauty, its music, its colors, its capacious balances, to each child as if that child were the only child in the world.

In my new school, I am frequently visited by former students. They come and sit as I teach, and now and then take a book down from our shelves and read. Skeeter came and borrowed a book on Greek history. His life is troubled at the edges, but his mind still yearns for knowledge and the radiance of facts. Many years ago (and I recall this with delight), as I left a bookshop on Columbus Avenue, a man in the throes of his addiction moved toward me in the way those who are on the verge of death do in this city in a pavanne of lamentation. He called out, "Ned, it's me, Jojo, remember me?" I embraced him. He grasped my hand and looked at me. He was bent and had to look up when he spoke: "You made me see myself as a hero and you gave me poetry." He wandered away into the breaking dark. It gathered him up.

I have never thought of life as an endless search for success. I have never known success — too much willfulness in my character. Everything hanging on the energy of my ego. The ways men and women seek peace and joy are multitudinous and strange indeed. So when I watch my former students, I want to see balance, delight, grace, hope, in their lives. And I do. They are fine parents, hard workers, dutiful citizens, churchgoers. They tell me they remember my schools as places of friendship, patience, silence, celebration. It is an accurate remembrance. We were small cloisters of peace and prayer, in a secular fashion, into which no clerical, political, governmental, or pedagogical banalities made incursions.

Hadrian says, in Marguerite Yourcenar's *Memoirs of Hadrian*, "When I seek deep within me for knowledge of myself, what I find is obscure, internal, unformulated, and as secret as any complicity."

"When I came to this city from upstate when I was eighteen, the city corrupted me," a mother told me. She spoke with candor, with uncorrupted honesty. She had read the text of her life. I have taught that skill to my children. She is in college now and has learned to savor learning.

So it is with six-year-old Gabriel, who left the Ricardo O'Gorman Garden in kindergarten to attend the Buckley School. He asked his teacher, in the midst of a math class, a question quite unrelated to math: "What is above the sky?" He had learned to let the mind fly. Nico writes his ballet teacher that his "turn out" gets better every day. Lillie loves being a funeral director. A worker in the Children's Storefront studies architecture. Ilika seeks his master's degree in horticulture. Others are teachers, bus drivers, civil servants, social workers, construction workers. On a cold winter day, in a driving snow, I heard my name called out from a bus that had stopped amid the traffic. Deshawn opened the door of the bus and greeted me. That was a splendid moment.

But my forty years in Harlem would be upended in a luxuriant harvest if our graduates and their children would find the time to struggle for justice, a moral elegance seldom seen in our society. It is as sweet as Bach, as good for the soul as Plato, and full of grace.

Poems

To the Memory of Lydia Hoffman

When she danced upon the counter of his bar in Flatbush,
her husband beat her, and she came to us bearing
a scar upon her cheek: she limped and wore a flaring
red hat with white flowers on the crown. I was
four months old and she drove me through
the nursery like a whip, oiled my crooked feet with
olive butter, and shined my father's hunting boots —
she was in our house like a furnace; she roots
now in my memory with the pikes of her agonies.
She devoured us: we ravaged her, left hoses running
in the gardens, and in the afternoon lay drumming
on the attic floor above her room where she rested,
after a morning of our barbarities. Lydia wept,
bent over tubs, baited traps, and prepared the meals:
we mauled her with cats, muddied shoes, and toads:

she studied us as a priest the victims in the sacred grove.
Lydia was born in Zurich in a farmhouse on the river Sihl.
When she was seven, the farm caught fire
and burned all day in the white pool of winter. As the pyre
reached to a skin of flame, at the moment the center
timber fell, her father rose up burning on the roof,
black and dumb and threw himself into the air
and fell spinning on the frozen ground:
his neck snapped and he thumped the ice. The sound
of a great wickedness pulled forever at her head,
and she dreamed of high flames on mountain tops,
of falling gables and a figure burning in the ruts
of a frozen field. She was queer, and hurled dishes
at my father, drank gin with straws, and sang the songs
of Heine in the kitchen. Lured by her fury to containment,
we learned the dark directives of her mind:
she was broody, lashed and crippled and heard the whine
of thugs in the maple grove, saw poisoned water
in the tap, smelt fire on the stairs. She raged
and cursed, limping through the halls, caged
in her agonies, her brow horned with scales of pain
that spat in the marrow of her legs. But in the spring,
when new wheat and cold streams heckle in the field
and animals break down the fences of their pens,
when field mice and vipers, cocks and hens
yield to the sun, Lydia led us to a hill
where we watched the world break its green egg
as she swung us, hopping in circles, on her game leg.
But as we grew older she grew mad and wandered
in the ice and weeds of winter nights, carrying
a lamp to seek a child she dreamed our father
burned and cast into the pool beside the barn,
where it lay swelled with toads. Our white farm

house was our priming shed and we were transformed
there into those who knew the ways extremity takes hold.
In her last days, upon a tilted bed, bold
as a withered kore, she was baptized and died with
a medal on her nightshirt in the odor of the holy oils.
She lay in her coffin clean as dough, hair in
ringlets, her nails painted red, a peacock power
croaking on the coming lights: from the cool tower
of her rest, she calls her father from the chars
of glory. But through the burned shadows and floating
timbers of the mind, Lydia walks, a peg-leg fury, bearing
the sorrow of a great compassion. She stomps her
foot above me, pulls up her sleeves, digs in her
heels, and swings the hook and grappling line
to strike the final mating blow
of the first calamities: of the father, the flaming rooftop,
    the gaping snows.

Great-Grandfather, Clam Diggers, and Homer

I

His family was like Spaniards
on horses; like prophets
their heads; superb with ladies;
bodies like cherry wood;
necks like chalices and eyes
that caught light as the sea
holds the sun; hunters who dreamed
the malediction of the fox.

But his youngest son, as the ellipse
describes the wave, in the skills
of discontent, drew masts down
the margins of books, callipered hulls
on his bedroom walls, for Poseidon
(rumored in tempests) laid his trident
like wings upon his eyes.

II

Though his father had no passion
for the sea, he built his son a boat
in the image of the one Odysseus
took to get away from Troy,
and one day, when a strong west wind
had touched the sound, his boy,
stripped to the sun and the oar's tug,

piloted that barge down the channel
to the sea and in Greek, pure
as the air that touches snow
(the sun of Asia glowed in the noise),
he read of the voyage through
the Dardanelles, past Sunium and Corinth
down the currents to Ithaca, where sunrise
and hot temples rose in the burning
noon, and the household waited
like traps in the timbered hall.

III

The clam diggers laughed: "What's this,
pressing through the morning?" "What noise,
what conspiracy? O Watch."

IV

At noonday, with bells and gulls
and white sail, a boy, arms red
with the hot light, and an old man,
singing, glided to the bottom
of the dock, where a groom pulled
with ropes Grecian music to a standstill.

Penelope, a flower, raised
her parasol and beckoned to the singer
to come up the stairway from the sea

into the blue air where a carriage
waited and a chestnut mare.

The boy who rowed the singer through
the waves, the salt air like a net
of marble on his back, laid his head upon
the oarlocks and dreamed of the light
on waves and Poseidon enthroned.

Childhood

Childhood is when the mouth tastes earth.
When the body is the body's sign;
when there is no studied end to time;
when hands join and make a cradle.

The child races through the snow in circles
and hears on the swing the sound of air;
the world's grave mummery is everywhere
and the sun like a falcon swerves toward his wrist.

There are drummers drumming and red sails
making April conquests in the bay;
the flesh is still a flurried sound of clay;
kites go as high as God and there are birds.

Though children are not passionate,
they feel the thigh against the sheet;
when there is thunder they will weep;
stairs go down to halls and rooms are darknesses.

The child is verb and hieroglyphic of his day
and sits and broods like a thinking flame;
that is called the playing of the game;
a child tends to glory like a pirate in a church.

And suffering fills him up with light
that holds its lumen for another time;
and one day as he plays he'll see a sign
and lift his arms and cry aloud like Man.

When I Would Love and Cannot Love

When I would love and cannot love,
then I know the rules of love
that render me complete and still.

In this new age redeemed by love,
I cannot dream of love and not awake
and dream of love again
even as I know that dream will
go when this new age,
redeemed by thunder from the fields, is still.

I am not of this opinion,
held by some I love,
that love is a fit of nerves
and vanishes, if it is ill begotten
in the world, like thunder into barns,
where the fields are sundered
from the rocks. I have this opinion:
love a cubit adds to my depth
and height and cannot go from me.

I have said, once when there seemed
just this exquisite joy,
followed by another and then another,
that love was this and
nothing other, but then I learned
that this love was each day

renewed,
as the thunder comes through
the ceiling when the storm is gone.

A Journey

I

I stood against the wall of your flesh
and yelped with hope that this was the holy
bonding that would loose the ash in
the ornamental trees and the seed pods
in the dry rock pools, that they might swarm
with decoration. My freed blood roamed
my sinew and brain like tar afire.

II

On the currents of my crabbed blood
I walked toward you like Eros split with rue.

III

Amish ladies cannot quilt bright colors
in the solitude of their rigid parlors,
but quilt in guarded kinship with other
ladies. This quilt, bright red triangles
and white, was thought perhaps a heater
of the blood, firing pin of the rested
nipple. Amish ladies would come out
of hiding to watch me cast off their quilt,
as I discover your creature body,
shape neither white triangle nor red

in this sewing room where thy flesh and mine
is scalloped, hemmed, pulled tight, patterned.

IV

Anemones, crows, wild rose, in the fleece
of salt caught in the air from the sea beyond
the marshes, each Doric pitch of stone,
had turned, in the ruby lymph of the scorched
sea's radiant face to fluted discs of flame.

(We had feasted there in Paestum on a bowl
of mushrooms and pasta in a sauce of herbs
and garlic with wine from the neighbor hills;
napkins white and damp, hemmed with green thread.)

But that light fell, when I turned to tell you
it had come, headlong into the fields, as if oxen
harnessed with ice had thudded against the sun.

V

The light on your face is sweet,
that rabid light that tolls
in my soul's garden like Eros's
idiot child.

VI

The Amish quilt lies
like a sail upon your
body. I search the wind
to move that sail, but
no wind comes from anywhere.

O that I might turn into
that wind and move that sail,
to be thy craft again,
thy body's bellied spinnaker.

Coda

*Hope is an orientation of the spirit, an orientation of the heart . . .
Hope is not the same as joy that things will go well, or will-
ingness to invest in enterprises that are obviously headed for
early success, but, rather, an ability to work for something because it is good . . .*

— Vaclav Havel

There is, in the desert I have inhabited since the beginning of my life, always reverberations of the harvest.
I am asked, now and then, what exactly have I been
doing in Harlem, these past forty years, building two
schools and spelling out the garbled, rambunctious
texts of my mad pilgrimage. There is no easy answer,
but this I do know: I have never set about to change
people's lives, to preach. I have done what I have done
to help, in my modest but heartfelt way, to build God's
kingdom on earth.

   I do not have any statistics of success or of failure
in the lives of the hundreds of children who have come

to my schools over the years. But there were more than a few moments of bright epiphanies during my trek in the desert: Nico, perfecting his "turn out" in ballet class; Mateo detecting a strain of Papageno's music in a Buxtehude cantata; the children in The Children's Storefront singing Handel; performing in *The Tempest* and *A Midsummer Night's Dream* (boiled down to their essential texts); and my pre-school scholars watching Cocteau's *La Belle et La Bête* for the first time and then, next day, asking to see it again.

I think I was perceived by many as a strange white intruder singing in the wind. If so, I sang with ferocity, and the children listened. I have written this book and tried to fill its pages with the remembrance of my life, from my earliest day in Southport to my all too short four decades in Harlem.

I hope this remembrance will be like a strong table built by a skilled carpenter and bear the weight upon it of many things.